How to Be
God's Little Princess

For more books by Sheila Walsh
Visit http:www.ThomasNelson.com.

How to Be God's Little Princess

Royal tips for manners,
etiquette, and true beauty

Sheila Walsh
with Jennifer Gerelds

Tommy NELSON®

A Division of Thomas Nelson Publishers

NASHVILLE   DALLAS   MEXICO CITY   RIO DE JANEIRO

HOW TO BE GOD'S LITTLE PRINCESS

© 2010 by Sheila Walsh

Sheila Walsh with Jennifer Gerelds

Illustrations by Jill Dubin

Published in Nashville, Tennessee, by Tommy Nelson. Tommy Nelson is a registered trademark of Thomas Nelson, Inc.

Published in association with the literary agency of Alive Communications, Inc. 7680 Goddard Street, Suite 200, Colorado Springs, CO 80920. www.alivecommunications.com

Thomas Nelson, Inc., titles may be purchased in bulk for educational, business, fund-raising, or sales promotional use. For information, please e-mail SpecialMarkets@ThomasNelson.com.

Unless otherwise noted, Scripture quotations are taken from the INTERNATIONAL CHILDREN'S BIBLE®. © 1986, 1988, 1999 by Thomas Nelson, Inc. All rights reserved.

Library of Congress Cataloging-in-Publication Data

Walsh, Sheila, 1956–
    How to be God's little princess : royal tips for manners, etiquette,
and true beauty / Sheila Walsh with Jennifer Gerelds.—1st ed.
        p. cm.
    ISBN 978-1-4003-1644-1 (hardcover : alk. paper)
    1. Girls—Conduct of life. 2. Girls—Religious life. 3. Beauty, Personal. 4.
Etiquette for children and teenagers. I. Gerelds, Jennifer. II. Title.
    BJ1651.W28 2010
    248.8'2—dc22
                                                                    2010045349

Mfr.: Quad Graphics/Fairfield, PA/August 2012/PPO# 136349

CONTENTS

Who is that young woman?
She shines out like the dawn.
She's as pretty as the moon.
She's as bright as the sun. . . .

Song of Solomon 6:10

THE PRINCESS WAY

Look in the mirror! Who is staring back? A princess. And she is you! You're growing up, life is changing, and you're excited to see what's going to happen next. At the same time, you're being placed in new—and sometimes confusing—situations. I'm sure there are some days when you feel like shouting out loud, "I love my life!" and other days when you want to crawl under the covers and not come out until Christmas.

Let's face it, being a princess is not as easy as some might think. What should you do if someone hurts your feelings? Or what if you are having a bad day and say something that you later regret? What is a princess to do?!

I have some wonderful news for you. That's where grace comes in. What is grace? Grace is God's free gift of unconditional love poured out on all His princesses. That means you are as loved on your good days as on your bad days. It means that there is nothing in the entire world that can keep you from God's love or keep His love from you. The best news of all is that when you are God's princess you don't have to get it right all the time. Being God's princess, is not about being perfect, it's about being perfectly loved. So whether you have all your ducks in a row or whether your ducks went to the fair, ate too much, and fell asleep—you are loved, you are loved, you are loved!

And now . . . drumroll, please . . . let's take a look at all the things a princess might need to know.

Sheila Walsh

Royal Advisors

Kindness, manners, and etiquette are tools to help you be self-confident in most situations. But how does a princess learn all these things? She turns to her royal advisors to help her know the perfect thing to do, say, and wear for every occasion. You have royal advisors too. Your advisors might be your mother or dad, or a grandmother or aunt, or all of them—seek out your royal advisors for answers. And discover the secrets of becoming a perfectly polite princess.

HOW TO DRESS LIKE A PRINCESS

A royal gown might be perfect for an elegant party, but it sure makes it difficult to skate. That's why, whenever possible, a princess considers where she's going and what she'll do before choosing her clothing, shoes, jewelry—even hairstyle. Then she makes sure everything is clean, fits, and is ready to go when she is.

The Lord makes me very happy. All that I am rejoices in my God. The Lord has covered me with clothes of salvation. He has covered me with a coat of goodness. . . .

ISAIAH 61:10

THE ROYAL WARDROBE

1. When a princess goes to a royal ball, she wears . . .
   a. Jeans and a T-shirt.
   b. A school uniform.
   c. A snorkel and fins.
   d. A beautiful ball gown.

2. When a princess goes to a school pizza party, she wears . . .
   a. A beautiful ball gown.
   b. Her robe and slippers.
   c. A large dog wrapped around her head.
   d. Jeans and a T-shirt.

3. When a princess goes to see a ballet on stage, she wears . . .
   a. A tutu.
   b. A leotard and tights.
   c. A bag of potato chips.
   d. Her nicest dress.

4. When a princess goes to an outside pool party, she wears . . .
   a. A leotard and tights.
   b. Boots, a heavy coat, and three hats.
   c. A costume.
   d. A swimsuit and cover-up.

Answers:

If your answer was always d, you're close to stepping out as a well-dressed princess! If you answered more a, b, or c—talk a little more to your royal advisors about dressing correctly for each occasion.

She's not dressed correctly for the activity.

DRESSING WITH A PRINCESS'S FLAIR

Every spring and fall try on clothes, hats, shoes, boots—everything. It's fun to start with your own closet before going out to look for new clothes. Ask your royal advisors to help you decide what still fits. Give whatever doesn't work for you to someone who could really use it.

Mix and match

Take what fits and pair it with other pieces in your closet. Start with a shirt. What goes best with it? Pants, jeans, maybe a skirt? If the top has a heavy pattern, stick to a solid color on the bottom; if the top has a solid color, try a pattern on the bottom.

If you are the more daring type and wear more mixed patterns, make sure the colors complement each other and that the pattern is bold only in one of the pieces.

Do you like layers? Try a contrasting tank top for a burst of color under an otherwise plain top.

Think colors

While looking in a mirror, use one color at a time and place it near your face. Does your face sparkle with bright bold colors, or do you look best in softer shades? Be sure to wear the colors that look best on you closest to your face. Wear the other colors as accents.

Go one color

Choose a "monochromatic" theme—that means using the same or shades of the same color, such as a light beige top with khaki pants. Add earth-tone accessories, and you end up with a subtly sophisticated result.

Jewelry and hair accessories

Choose earrings (if you wear them), necklaces, or bracelets that will look good with your outfit. Remember, it's the details such as barrettes, hairbands, belts, leggings, and even shoelaces that can help bring the whole outfit together.

For example, a plaid hairband with a little hot pink and blue might tie together the hot pink in your top with your blue denim skirt. Or your earrings might be the same color as your shoes or belt. Throughout the outfit, find ways to use some of the same colors.

Purse, backpack, cinch sack

Purses are meant to be practical, but don't try to pack everything you own in one. Keep it simple as you find a bag that suits your style, colors, the season, and the occasion. For the royal ball, you'd take a small fancy purse; to school an everyday purse, bag, or backpack that suits your style; to a theme park or waterpark choose something that you won't lose on the roller coaster and allows your hands to be free, such as a cinch sack or even an outfit with pockets.

Boots, sandals, sneakers ...

And the list goes on. Footwear is where function meets fashion —but be careful: it's difficult to smile when your feet hurt! Try to keep the colors neutral or match them to your outfit, unless you just go for colorful shoes. And no matter what the season, keep your feet and shoes clean.

Being modest

You can dress in high fashion and still remain modest, if you follow some of the these royal tips:

- Wear leggings under skirts that run too short.
- Wear longer T-shirts or tanks with low-rise pants.
- Try skinny jeans from the boys' department that have a higher waist.

- Raise arms up high to test shirts for being too short.
- Check the cut of armholes and necklines so that bra straps don't show.

Step back

After you've put your outfit together, take a final look at the finished product. Then, standing in front of a mirror, close your eyes, count to ten, then open your eyes. Did anything pop out at you? Perhaps your shoes are too bright? If so, consider changing them. And be sure to ask your royal advisor's opinion too.

TIE-DYE

Ready to show your true colors? If you have dye and just a little daring, you can create your own kaleidoscope of color on shirts, hats, scarves, towels, and . . . well, just about anything that starts off white. Ask your royal advisors for help. Then follow these steps to a fun and creative wardrobe.

Tie-Dye a spiral shirt
✓ **What you'll need**
☐ white cotton T-shirts
☐ soda ash[†]
☐ rubber bands
☐ procion dye[†]
☐ rubber or plastic gloves
☐ eye goggles
☐ squirt bottles
☐ a plastic container (tub)

[†]Soda ash and procion dye are available in most fabric and craft stores. Other dyes might not give you a tie-dye effect.

1. Wash and dry your shirt.
2. Lay shirt flat. Pinch up fabric and swirl slightly. Tie rubber band around the base of the swirl. Repeat this pattern until you have as many bands as you want.
3. Dip entire shirt into soda ash solution. (Mix ½ cup of soda ash fixer for every gallon of water. Be sure to wear gloves and eye goggles for protection.)
4. Follow dye directions on label (usually around 1 tablespoon of dye for every 16 ounces of water). If you just want one color, dip entire shirt in a tub with the dye solution. If you'd like multiple colors, put each color of dye into its own squirt bottle and squirt each color wherever you want it on the shirt.
5. Let the dye soak in for several hours.
6. Finally, remove the bands and wash the shirt in hot water.
7. Congratulations! You've just created your first tie-dye shirt. Now that you know the basics, you can experiment with design patterns, colors, and fabrics.

My royal notes:

FLASHIN' FASHION

Are you Flashy and Fabulous? Pretty but Practical? Sharp but Safe? Take this quiz to find out your style today—of course, that could change tomorrow.

1. When you walk into a clothing store, you feel . . .
   a. Bored
   b. Overwhelmed
   c. Excited

2. Which of these colors grabs your attention the most?
   a. Black
   b. Pale Pink
   c. Bright yellow

3. When you need an outfit, you . . .
   a. Buy the one the mannequin is wearing.
   b. Ask Mom for help.
   c. Put it together yourself.

4. When it comes to accessories, your motto is:
   a. Why bother?
   b. Less is more.
   c. The more the merrier.

5. The kind of outfit you like should . . .
   a. Be suitable for your activity.
   b. Help you blend in.
   c. Stand out in the crowd.

If you answered mostly . . .

    a—you're Pretty but Practical. You may have a style, but fashion is definitely not your focus.

    b—you're Sharp but Safe. You might not be setting any trends, but you're also not making any mistakes. You might feel unsure at first, but after some encouragement from your friends, you love sporting your style.

    c—you're Flashy and Fabulous. Not everybody can wear that hat and those leggings and get away with it, but you can! The more unusual and outrageous the ensemble, the more it catches your eye. But you also know the limits.

Pretty
but
Practical

Sharp
but
Safe

Flashy
and
Fabulous

FASHION FORWARD

Want something unique? Whether it's jewelry, something to wear, or a gift, show your own sense of style by designing your own creations.

✓ **What you'll need**
- ☐ wire, thin
- ☐ dental floss*, string, or embroidery thread
- ☐ glue
- ☐ beads, or other items you can string
- ☐ a tape measure
- ☐ scissors
- ☐ special items listed under each project
  Optional: For added color use paints, glitter, rhinestones, ribbon, or small fun things you've found at garage sales and flea markets.

*Dental floss is stronger than most threads.

Bangle bracelets

Wrap the tape measure loosely around your wrist as many times as you'd like your bracelet to wrap. To the total, add 5 inches. That is the amount of wire you'll need for one bracelet. Loop and wrap one end of the wire around a bead to keep the beads from falling off. String the beads (or other items) leaving enough wire at the end to loop, weave back through the last beads, and wrap securely. Take one end and wrap it loosely around your wrist. The bracelet should be easy to slide on and off.

Paper beads

For these, you'll also need colorful magazines and toothpicks. Start by drawing long, thin triangles. Cut out the triangles. Starting with the widest end, wrap a triangle around a toothpick. Glue the tip. Once the glue has dried, carefully remove the toothpick. Repeat until you have all the beads that you need for your jewelry. To decorate beads, paint or add glitter. To make large beads, use a soda straw or a long, thin twig or stick. To make a necklace, thread the beads onto some dental floss and tie securely.

Book Bag charms

For this project you'll also need a key ring. Use dental floss or embroidery thread as string. Measure the string the length you want your charms to dangle from the key ring. Now add about 5 inches. String the beads (or other items) leaving enough length at the end to tie a knot large enough to hold the beads in place. Then tie the charm to the key ring. Repeat to make as many as you want to dangle from your book bag. Use this same technique to make charms for other items, such as your phone.

Community project

If you enjoy making jewelry, ask other princesses (even princes) in your church to help make jewelry as a fund-raising project.

BEACH BEAUTIES

Heaven and earth should praise him.
The seas and everything in them should also.

PSALM 69:34

Shell necklace
✓ **What you'll need**
- ☐ shells
- ☐ clear fingernail polish
- ☐ colored fingernail polish
- ☐ permanent markers
- ☐ string

    Optional: beads, glitter glue.

When you're at the beach, look for the ribbed bivalve shells that already have a hole drilled in the top (courtesy of another sea creature that drilled the hole to get to the clam . . . but was too busy or too full to make a necklace); or buy them at a hobby or craft store. Wash the shells, then decorate them.

For example: You might paint one a solid color. After it dries, apply polka dots, stripes, a cross, a flower, or whatever design you like. Paint a layer of clear fingernail polish as a topcoat to protect the finish.

Cut necklace string long enough to fit around your head. Add about 5 inches. Holding both ends of string in one hand, force the center of string through the shell's hole and pull the loop out about an inch. Then thread the two ends through the loop and pull through to make a knot. Place around your neck and fit to the length you'd like. (Be sure you can put it on over your head.) Tie a knot.

Sand dollar delights
Instead of painting on paper, put your designs on beautiful sand dollars to use on purses or belts, wear as jewelry, decorate your room, or make a Christmas ornament. Be sure

to sign your work! (I wonder if the famous painter Picasso began like this? Hmm.)

✓ **What you'll need**
☐ sand dollars*
☐ acrylic paint
☐ glitter glue
☐ yarn or string

Paint a solid basecoat on each sand dollar. When dry, create a sunset or beach scene (or whatever you like) using acrylic paint. Top with clear acrylic paint or glitter glue for a shimmery effect. To use as a necklace or ornament, thread a hole with yarn or string. Remember to match the size of the sand dollar to how you will use it: larger for a wall hanging; smaller for a necklace.

*If you find the sand dollars in the ocean, you will have to soak them in a water and bleach solution overnight. Let them dry in the sun until bleached white.

THE RUNWAY FAVORITE

The fashion shows of Paris and New York are filled with the latest beautiful styles—and also some of the most outlandish designs ever created. For your runway show before the royal court, explore your own creativity as you design with beauty in mind—or go for the wildest and wackiest combinations you can conceive. Either way, you might be surprised at how great you look when you just have fun!

Backstage
1. Choose a small number of girl guests.
2. It's great if your guests all have dance leotards (and

tights) to wear, but if not, swimsuits or other close-fitting clothes will work too.

3. Ask each guest to bring some scarves, jewelry, shoes, purses, hats, sweaters, shirts. . . . (Your mothers, sisters, grandmothers, and aunts might have some things you could borrow or perhaps take a trip to the local thrift store.)

4. When each guest arrives take her picture with (or write down the items) she brought—so you'll be sure each item goes home with the right guest.

5. Sort everyone's items by type (jewelry with jewelry, scarves with scarves).

6. Divide into groups of two or more. One girl will be a designer, the other girl(s) will be the model. Then switch so the model is the designer, the designer is the model—until everyone has had a turn doing both parts.

7. If possible, have the models out of view so no one but the model's designer sees her outfit before the show. Then the designers join the audience.

The show

8. Set up an area as a runway. It can be elaborate. It can be simple. (Ask your royal advisors.)

9. Set up some chairs near the runway.

10. Once everyone is dressed and the designer(s) is seated in the audience, put on some music and start the show. Choose music suitable for a princess—so no elephants playing trombones!

11. Each model makes a grand entrance, pauses, then walks down the runway. As she walks the runway, her designer briefly describes the look.

12. Repeat until everyone has been both a model and a designer.

You'll want to serve food and drinks to your guests. Ask your royal advisors for ideas on when and what to serve.

HOW TO
WEAR A TIARA
(and other princess necessities)

Have you ever wondered why princesses wear tiaras (small half-crowns)? They are the international symbol of royalty! You can have fun making, trying on, and wearing different tiaras that show your special style. But God says the most beautiful crown can't be made with human hands. God alone can place a crown on our heads with His wisdom. Ask Him for wisdom in your prayers.

> *Believe in the value of wisdom, and it will make*
> *you great. Use it, and it will bring honor to you.*
> *Like flowers in your hair, it will beautify your life.*
> *Like a crown, it will make you look beautiful.*

PROVERBS 4:8–9

THE RIGHT TIARA FOR YOU

Tiaras come in many shapes, sizes, and styles. What's important is that the tiara frames your face. But because no one's face is absolutely round, oval, long, or full, you'll need to try on tiaras to see which style looks best on you.

Remember, if your hair is up, wear your tiara back from your face, set directly in front of or pushed into your hair; if your hair is down, wear your tiara closer to your face as you would a headband.

If your face is . . .	Choose a tiara . . .
Round	with a high peak in the center.
Oval	that fits like a headband and is low to the head.
Rectangle	that goes from side to side (ear to ear), stays close to the head, and has a small center peak.
Square	that has a V shape at the top, like a heart.
Heart-shaped	with multiple heights like a staircase.
Diamond	that is almost any shape.
Inverted Triangle	narrow at the sides and fuller in the center.
Triangle	that has high sides almost equal to the center and goes from side to side (ear to ear)

Match the tiara to the face shape it frames best.

Round

Square

Inverted Triangle

Oval

Heart-shaped

Rectangle

Diamond

Triangle

1

2

3

4

5

6

7

8

Answers: round 2, square 3, inverted triangle 7, oval 5, heart-shaped 8, rectangle 1, diamond 6, triangle 4.

HAIR JEWELRY

Princesses wear many types of jewelry, so when a traditional tiara won't work, try one of these jeweled hair decorations.

Backpiece

Wear this when you want to kick it up a notch without overdoing the outfit. It fits like a barrette by pulling a portion of your hair to the back of your head or is tucked into a more formal French twist. Wear the casual ones almost anytime, but save the super-ornate ones for those special occasions.

Combs and hairpins

Combs and hairpins serve a similar function as a backpiece. Both can be used to pull the hair back and keep it in position. Again, save the fancier pieces for formal events.

Jewel-studded headbands

Great for casual events. A headband can be worn with jeans almost anywhere. This type of headband works well when long hair is worn down and on most short hair.

Jewel-studded double headbands

Perfect for a formal event or just a trip to the movies. Wear this flexible headband as a tiara by tilting it slightly forward, or as a decorative headband, or wrapped around an updo or ponytail.

V-band

A type of tiara that sits lightly on the forehead in a V shape. Usually worn to more formal events.

❓
WHAT'S WRONG WITH THIS PICTURE?

She's wearing too much hair jewelry.

THE "MANE" EVENT

Long or short, soft or springy, black or fiery red, our hair—whichever kind God gave us—is a colorful canvas we carry with us everywhere we go. But why bother leaving it blank? With just a little creativity, you can make your own accessories to further express your unique personality—just be sure the glue is dry before wearing your creation, or you might still be wearing it to college.

✓ **What you'll need**
- ☐ plastic headbands (yes, the cheap kind)
- ☐ ribbon
- ☐ different fabrics (preferably the kinds that don't unravel when cut)
- ☐ floral wire and needle nose pliers
- ☐ hot glue and gun or regular white glue
- ☐ buttons, beads, or any decorative items you can glue

To make a ribbon band, start with a dot of hot glue at the base of the band. Begin wrapping the ribbon around the band, overlapping the edges and winding up like the ridges on a screw. Once the band is completely wrapped, glue the end of the ribbon to the inside bottom part of the band.

Now, add your creativity. You could:

- Glue hot pink buttons onto a black ribbon or plastic band.
- Craft a homemade flower out of leather-type fabric. Cut out a circle to act as a base. Then cut petals and glue the inside edges to the circle base. Layer another row of petals on top of the first. Finish

with a sparkly gem on the inside (as the center of the flower and to hide the glued tips). Use glue combined with floral wire to attach the flower to the band.

For Plastic Headbands
- Roll the band in white glue and add solid-color glitter or apply in stripes.
- Sew or glue a fabric sleeve. Scrunch it up for a layered look. Glue the ends to keep it in place.

For barrettes and hair clips, just keep your ribbon, beads, and glue handy. Try combining them, with a bottom layer of ribbon topped with coordinating beads or buttons. Let your imagination run wild!

A REGAL WAVE

A princess often has occasion to wave to the public—sometimes for hours. If she makes a big wave bending her wrist, she'd quickly be back at the castle with her wrist in a silver bucket of ice. *Ouch!* That's why a princess uses a more subtle wave. Try it!

Bend your right elbow so your fingers point to the ceiling. With your wrist straight, your palm facing forward, and your fingers touching, gently move your wrist and hand so your thumb almost points behind you. Now move it back the way you started.

To complete the wave in a parade, you would look to the people you are waving to on the right and smile. Keep your left hand resting in your lap. Then switch and look to the left side and wave with your left hand. Rest your right hand in your lap. Never wave with both hands at the same time . . . or you might look like you are trying to attract attention because you've lost your dog!

HOW A PRINCESS PERFECTS HER POISE

Don't be confused: being poised and confident doesn't mean you're boastful. It means you are comfortable being a child of the King! Remember when you walk in His ways, you possess all the poise and confidence you need to show the world how royally grand it is to be in God's family!

You are young, but do not let anyone treat you as if you were not important. Be an example to show the believers how they should live. Show them with your words, with the way you live, with your love, with your faith, and with your pure life.

1 TIMOTHY 4:12

BOLD OR BASHFUL?

Are you the kind of princess who welcomes adventure or who waits quietly in court? Take this quiz to find out your type.

1. When you walk into a crowded classroom, you . . .
   a. Look down and stay as close to the wall as possible.
   b. Look for a friend you know before going any farther.
   c. Look for an opening so you can jump in and start talking.

2. When the teacher asks for volunteers, you . . .
   a. Stare at your desk.
   b. Try to become invisible.
   c. Raise your hand really high.

3. When you have to talk in front of the class, you . . .
   a. Hate it.
   b. Like it.
   c. Love it.

4. When you meet someone new, you . . .
   a. Look down and stay quiet.
   b. Look her in the eyes, smile, and say hello.
   c. Smile, reach out to shake hands with her, and get a conversation going.

5. When your mom wants you to take up a new sport or hobby, you . . .
   a. Complain that you don't know how to do it.
   b. Agree, but feel nervous inside.
   c. Jump up and down in excitement and thanks.

Tally Up!

Write in the blanks how many of each letter you chose:

a_____ b_____ c_____

If you had 3 or more

a answers: You are a Bashful Beauty. New people and experiences can make you nervous. Remember that God, your King, loves a gentle and quiet spirit. He can give you the courage to be bold for Him.

b answers: You are a Power Princess. You might not always want center stage, but you know how to keep the show going. Your quiet confidence helps keep your class and home ticking like clockwork. God says the one who is faithful in the small things will be faithful in the big things too!

c answers: You're a Daring Diva. You look adventure in the eye and laugh with delight. People flock to you, and you lead by your bold excitement. Remember that God says to wait on Him for His direction and lead. And don't forget that your real strength comes from God. Use your boldness to encourage and help others.

Two or less of each: You're a Peaceful Princess. You rule with a steady scepter. You can be bold or quiet, outgoing or shy depending on the situation. Don't be afraid to be the real you. Ask God for wisdom to help you be all that He made you to be.

STRAIGHT TALK

Sit up straight and walk tall, and you'll look regal in everything you do. You'll also breathe, think, look, and feel better—all because you'll be fueling your body with more oxygen.

What's the secret to a good posture?

Human backs are meant to be in a natural S-like shape—not straight as a board. Pretend you are a puppet with strings attached to your head and backbone. When you are standing or sitting, the strings are from the ceiling; when you are lying down, the strings attach to the wall.

Now make an exaggerated slouch. Pretend someone is gently pulling the strings and, as she does, your head and back slowly pull to a straight position.

Can you hold that position for long? If not, talk to one of your royal advisors about ways to strengthen the muscles in your torso (back and front).

A princess sits as far back in a chair as possible to help her sit straighter.

WHAT'S WRONG WITH THIS PICTURE?

She's not sitting properly or modestly.

A GRAND ENTRANCE

Now that you're standing tall, you're ready to face the public with refined style. Just picture your favorite princess stepping into a room filled with people. Does she hide? Is she shy? No! She's the princess, and her every move says so. Now what about you? Remember, you're a princess too! Follow these royal reminders to make your entrance grander than ever.

1. Shoulders back; back straight.
2. Head up, looking out (but try not to fall over the cat!).

3. Think regal thoughts. The more confident you feel about yourself, the stronger your presence will be. You are, after all, a child of the King!

4. Smile! It will put you and everyone else at ease.

5. Remember that we live to give glory to God, not ourselves. So look for ways you can serve and encourage the others around you in Christ!

Kindness and manners help a princess fit in everywhere—and that's exactly where you'll find God's princesses . . . everywhere.

quiz
PRINCESS POWER

*When you do things, do not let selfishness or
pride be your guide. Be humble and give more
honor to others than to yourselves.*

PHILIPPIANS 2:3

Princesses have power—power to build others up. God wants His princesses to reign with kindness and compassion. Take this quiz to find out if you are a princess powerhouse!

1. The cookies are almost gone. One is left on the plate, and you know your brother hasn't had one. However, he's in another room and doesn't know Mom made cookies. You . . .
   a. Rejoice in your good fortune as you gobble up every last crumb.
   b. Divide the cookie in half and take the other half to your brother.

c. Call your brother in to the kitchen so he can eat the cookie.

2. You just received your favorite game for your birthday. Your friends whom you invited over for your slumber party are happy for you too. You . . .
   a. Put the game aside so that you can play with everyone at the same time.
   b. Play the game for a little while, letting your friends watch and take turns.
   c. Sit on the couch and play by yourself, forgetting about everyone else.

3. Your friend walks over to you where you are talking with a group of girls. Suddenly, you notice that her zipper is down. You . . .
   a. Laugh out loud and point while saying something embarrassing.
   b. Pretend you didn't see anything.
   c. Pull her aside for a moment and quietly tell her the problem so she can fix it without embarrassment.

4. Your mom has had a hard day taking care of your little sister, helping you with homework, and getting dinner ready. You notice that your sister's toys are still all over the floor, but you want to go outside to play. You . . .
   a. Bolt for the door and hope to escape to the backyard without anyone noticing you.
   b. Take a moment to pick up the toys and put them in the right place before heading outside.
   c. Tell your little sister that she needs to pick up her toys as you go outside to play.

5. Your dad is on the phone talking to someone about work. The computer won't connect to the Internet and you need help getting it online again to do your homework. You . . .
   a. Start saying your father's name louder and louder until you get his attention, using cymbals if necessary.
   b. Decide you have the perfect excuse to skip your homework and go outside to play.
   c. Ask your mom or other family member to help you.

Tally up!
Add your points using the following answer key.
What does your score say about your servant heart?

Answer Key
1. a=0 points, b=1 point, c=2 points
2. a=2 points, b=1 point, c=0 points
3. a=0 points, b=1 point, c=2 points
4. a=0 points, b=2 points, c=1 point
5. a=0 points, b=0 points, c=2 points

Power House: Scored 8–10. Congratulations! You use your princess power to serve and love others well.

Power Surge: Scored 5–7. Not bad! You have moments of strength and weakness. Exercise those spiritual muscles by looking for more opportunities to put others in front of yourself.

Power Outage: Scored 0–4. Selfishness has reduced your strength! Power up by serving others. Every day ask yourself, who does God want me to help today?

A princess doesn't correct others' manners.

BLUSHED AND BEAUTIFUL

Oh, no! You've made a mistake! Are you still a princess? Absolutely, you won't lose your place in the kingdom. Just be honest and admit it. Check out these potentially embarrassing moments—and the ways a princess would react!

Tongue-tied
Have you ever tried to talk, but found that the wrong words came out? Maybe you switched the letters, said the wrong word altogether, or blurted out the one thing you didn't mean to say. Then maybe someone giggles and you turn red. What should you do?

A princess would admit she was tongue-tied. After all, it happens to everyone. Then laugh with her friends until she could get her tongue unstuck.

Wrong answer
You were so sure you knew the answer to your teacher's question. But you were wrong! Now you are so embarrassed you want to crawl under the desk and dig your way to the other side of the world. What should you do?

A princess knows no one is expected to know all the answers and that being wrong in class is all part of learning. The important thing is that you listened and participated.

Birthday blunders
Your best friend's birthday came and went. You forgot all about it! What should you do?

A princess would give her a heartfelt apology and give her a present or card anyway.

Fall out

You are walking down the street, trip, and fall flat on the ground. What should you do?

A princess would brush herself off and check for injuries. Then look around and, instead of blushing, try to do something funny or laugh. She might just take a bow, as if she'd just given the best falling performance ever. Then smile, tell everyone that there will be another show at 8:00 p.m., and move on!

Belching or worse

You're sitting at the table when suddenly it happens: air, uninvited by you, makes its great escape out your mouth (or worse, the other end). It's too late to take it back, and too loud to pretend it didn't happen. What should you do?

A princess who burped would cover her mouth with her napkin (or hand) and softly say, "Excuse me." If it came from the other end, she'd pretend it never happened, as should the others around her. She would never point to someone else and say, "He did it!"

---

quiz

MEETING MANNERS METER

Take this quiz to rank your princess politeness. Then polish up whatever needs it most!

1. Your best friend brings a new friend to Sunday school. You . . .
   a. Smile and ask her name.

   b. Become secretly mad that your friend is hanging out with someone else.

   c. Play with the people you already know.

2. You have just joined a new club, and you arrive for the first meeting. You . . .
   a. Scan the room looking for anyone you know to talk to.
   b. Take the first empty seat and start talking to whoever is beside you.
   c. Look down at your desk and wait for someone to say something to you.

3. Your dad wants to introduce you to some of his coworkers. You . . .
   a. Ignore him as you look for low-flying hamsters.
   b. Keep asking when you can leave because you are bored.
   c. Stand quietly by his side and smile. After he introduces you to his friends, you say, "Nice to meet you."

4. At school, you notice a new girl who seems to be from another country. You . . .
   a. Pretend that you didn't see her.
   b. Make fun of her with your friends.
   c. Go up to her and try to make her feel welcome.

5. You've almost made it to the final level on your game when the phone rings. You . . .
   a. Pause your game and answer the phone with a polite, "Hello."
   b. Let it ring while you keep playing until you lose all your lives.
   c. Yell for your mom to get the phone.

Answers: Starting at the bottom, color in one rectangle on the meter for each correct answer:

MEETING METER

Master	
Apprentice	
Novice	

THE HIGHS AND LOWS OF MALL MANNERS

Did the sale already start? Can't wait to reach your favorite store in the mall? Before you start bowling over shoppers in your excitement, check out these helpful tips when making your way through the crowds.

Escalator Know-How
A princess knows that while escalators may seem like a small version of an amusement park ride, they really are not designed for that level of fun. When you take an escalator, be sure to:

- Keep shoelaces and fingers away from the stairs.
- Find your spot on the right side and stay in it all the way up or down.

⚛ WHAT'S WRONG WITH THIS PICTURE?

The dancing girl is not using good manners on an escalator.

Elevator envy

What is it about elevators that makes even the quietest princess come alive with excitement? A princess remembers to:

- Face the doors that will open so that you can exit without tripping.
- If a young child wants to push the button, be gracious, step back, and let the child push it. Remember, you used to be that child!

- Everyone can hear you, so put your previous conversation on hold—particularly if it involves any personal topics, such as why your dog has bad breath.
- Move to the side or back as others enter or exit—but try to stay near your friends.
- Use the elevator's phone or panic button only in an emergency.
- If you ever feel uncomfortable riding an elevator, don't ride it.

Mall etiquette

- Be safe and stay with the people who brought you to the mall.
- Be patient with others who might take longer to order or pay.
- Be aware of those who have difficulties walking, and do not trip over their cane or crutches.

> A princess doesn't shout or run in a mall.

Stay safe

- Don't talk to strangers.
- If you get lost, find a mom with kids to help you.
- Know the cell number(s) of the person you are with at the mall.
- Know your mom and dad's cell, home, and work numbers. If you have trouble remembering them, write them down on a card to keep in your purse or pocket.

HANDLING DOORS AND CHAIRS WITH DIGNITY

Your family has just arrived at a restaurant. Your dad opens the car door (as a good gentleman would), and waits for you to exit. What do you do?

- You could keep playing your video game or reading your book—but then you might go to bed hungry.
- A better choice would be to stop everything and get out right away.
- The best choice would be to look him in the eyes and say, "Thank you!", smile, and gracefully get out of the car.

Before you reach the restaurant entrance with your family, another family walks up. What should you do?

- Well, you could rush ahead to be first, but you'll likely feel a little foolish. More than that, Jesus is pretty big on putting others in front of ourselves.
- A better choice would be to let the other family pass in front. And the little bit of waiting makes the food taste that much better!
- The best choice of all would be to hold the door open so that the other family could pass through. Your servant spirit will inspire them and greatly please your Savior who's watching!

Now you're finally inside. Fortunately, there is a chair still available while you wait for an open table. As you settle in for what you hope is a short wait, you notice an older woman and your mom are left standing. What happens now?

- You could keep sitting, close your eyes, and pretend no one else exists.
- A better choice would be to offer your chair to your mom.
- The best choice: Ask the women standing if one would like to sit. Show them your sincerity by standing up and moving out of the way so that one of them can accept your offer. Remember, God sees even our smallest acts of kindness and can use them to show others His love.

HOW TO BE FRIENDS PRINCESS STYLE

Finding a good friend is like choosing a good book—sometimes you have to look beyond the covers to find what's truly valuable inside. And becoming a great friend is the first step to finding one. Work at good communication, invest your time, overlook offenses, and pray for God's blessing as you seek to find and maintain the relationships God has for you.

> . . . If we love each other, God's love has
> reached its goal. It is made perfect in us.
>
> 1 JOHN 4:12

WHAT'S YOUR PRINCESS FRIENDSHIP STYLE?

You get a real lift from hanging out with your friends. But what kind of friend are you? Take this quiz to see if your friendship style soars or stays stuck in the ground.

1. When I talk to my friend, we mostly talk about . . .
   a. Whatever is going on in each of our lives.
   b. Clothes or boys.
   c. The latest rumor about other girls.

2. When my best friend wins an award, I . . .
   a. Feel excited for her and tell her, "Congratulations!"
   b. Wish it had been me who had won.
   c. Act happy but don't really care because I'm interested in other things.

3. If another person starts to make fun of my friend, I . . .
   a. Laugh at the joke because I want to fit in.
   b. Get quiet but don't say anything. Inside I feel badly about it.
   c. Frown and tell the person to stop saying bad things about my friend.

4. Your friend tells you a secret, and you promise not to tell. Yet, you know lots of people who'd love to hear it. You decide to . . .
   a. Tell one or two of your very closest friends.
   b. Keep the secret and not say a word.
   c. Share it as a prayer request in Sunday school so that everyone can know.

5. You and a friend are at a party, but everyone is watching a movie your friend is not allowed to see.

You decide to . . .

a. Tell her that her parents are too strict. It's a perfectly fine movie, anyway.

b. Tell her to watch it, but you'll cover her eyes during the bad parts.

c. Sit upstairs and hang out with her while the others watch the movie.

So what's your friendship level?

High and Mighty: 8–10 points

Hobbling but Hopeful: 5–7 points

In the Hole: 0–4 points

FRIENDSHIP FOCUS

*Many people claim to be loyal. But it is hard to
find someone who really can be trusted.*

PROVERBS 20:6

Every princess knows for almost every good thing, someone has to put forth a little effort—and it's no different with
friends. If you want a good friend, you have to work at being
a good friend yourself. Here's how!

> A princess looks for the God-given talent in everyone.

Take a look at yourself
No one is perfect, but to be a good friend you should be
aiming for the following character qualities:

- Are you a Christian? Be sure others can tell by the
  way you talk, dress, and act.
- Are you thoughtful? Serve others and listen to what
  they say.
- Are you real around your friends? Stay around
  friends where you are your true self.
- Are you optimistic? Try to see the best in people
  and circumstances.
- Are you giving off the right vibe? Look people in
  the eyes and smile! If you're looking down or away,
  people may think you don't like them.
- Are you trustworthy, dependable, kind? You'll never
  regret doing the right thing.
- Are you forgiving? Everyone makes mistakes, be
  generous in your forgiveness.

Make the first move

Don't wait around for someone to call or e-mail you. Pick up the phone to talk or to invite a friend over. At school or church, be the first one to walk over and say, "Hi!" You could be God's answer to someone else's prayer for a good friend too!

Keep it rolling

Finding friends is only half the battle. Unless you're seeing them every day at school, the hectic pace of life can dim the connection. To keep your friendship strong, consider doing the following:

- Find a time each week to call or write a note just to stay in touch.
- Schedule times to get together. It may require prodding your parents, but they can help you set aside time for friends.
- Go below the surface. When you do get a chance to hang out, it's okay to talk about general stuff at first, like weather or your new wardrobe. But don't let it stay there. Ask how she's getting along with her family and teachers, or ask her about whatever God's been teaching her lately. The idea is to get to know her for who she is and not just what she wears or does.

True friendships

Read the traits on page 42 again, but this time with your friends in mind. Be sure they are aiming toward the same character qualities.

SECRET MESSAGE

Match the number with its letter. The first word is done for you.

Code		
A=1	B=2	C=3
D=4	E=5	F=6
G=7	H=8	I=9
J=10	K=11	L=12
M=13	N=14	O=15
P=16	Q=17	R=18
S=19	T=20	U=21
V=22	W=23	X=24
Y=25	Z=26	

E V E R Y   ___ ___ ___ ___ ___ ___ ___ ___   ___ ___ ___ ___ ___
5 22 5 18 25   16 18 9 14 3 5 19 19   11 14 15 23 19

___ ___ ___   ___ ___   ___ ___ ___ ___
8 15 23   20 15   13 1 11 5

___   ___ ___ ___ ___ ___   ___ ___ ___ ___ ___
1   7 18 1 14 4   6 9 18 19 20

___ ___ ___ ___ ___ ___ ___ ___ ___ ___
9 13 16 18 5 19 19 9 15 14

Answer: Every princess knows how to make a grand first impression.

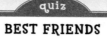

BEST FRIENDS

Understanding a person's thoughts is as hard as getting water from a deep well. But someone with understanding can find the wisdom there.

PROVERBS 20:5

You both say you're best friends. But how well do you know each other? First, answer these questions about your friend. Then ask her the questions to find out the real answers. Then have her do the same for you. Check the power level of your connection below.

1. My best friend's favorite color is _____.
   (Her answer:_____)
2. Her favorite after-school activity is _____.
   (Her answer:_____)
3. Her pets' names are _____. (Her answer:_____)
4. Her eye color is _____. (Her answer:_____)
5. Her birthday is _____. (Her answer:_____)
6. When she grows up she wants to be _____.
   (Her answer:_____)
7. What embarrasses her the most is:_____.
   (Her answer:_____)
8. The funniest movie she's ever seen is _____.
   (Her answer:_____)
9. She likes life to be: a) calm and predictable, b) wild and adventurous, c) somewhere in between.
   (Her answer:_____)
10. She considers herself to be: a) outgoing, b) shy, c) somewhere in between. (Her answer:_____)

Friendship Power Level
   Fully charged: 8–10 matches
   Low wattage: 5–7 matches
   Disconnected: 4 or below

THE POSITIVE PRINCESS

So comfort each other and give each other
strength, just as you are doing now.

1 Thessalonians 5:11

Well, guess what?! God has called you to be a cheerleader! Don't worry, you don't even have to try out. He has given you all the skills you need. His Holy Spirit works inside you to fuel your energy and excitement for God and His people. Your main job is to cheer others on in the Lord!

What's all the excitement?

You might wonder why we need to be encouraging other Christians. If you come from a Christian home, attend church, and everything is going well in your life—then obeying God might seem easy to you. But if your parents don't know the Lord, you learn about God on your own, or something sad or bad has happened in your life—obeying God might seem difficult.

God says that hard times come into everyone's life. God uses the tough stuff to turn our hearts toward Him, but sometimes in anger or frustration Christians can be tempted to turn away from God. They might forget all of His goodness. They might only be able to see the problem and not the answer.

Get in the game

That's where God's cheerleaders come into play. We can come alongside our friends and encourage them with the truth. Of course, you won't be saying silly cheers to build them up. You'll strengthen them through your loyal friendship. Cry with them when they're sad. Hug them when they need a touch. And at the right time, tell them that God does love them. Remind them of all His precious promises.

Here are a few that could be helpful:

2 Kings 20:5: This is what the Lord, the God of your ancestor David, says: I have heard your prayer. And I have seen your tears. So I will heal you.

Jeremiah 29:11–12: I have good plans for you. I don't plan to hurt you. I plan to give you hope and a good future. Then you will call my name. Then you will come to me and pray to me. And I will listen to you.

Romans 8:28: We know that in everything God works for the good of those who love him.

Psalm 139:5: You are all around me—in front and in back. You have put your hand on me.

BRIGHTEN A FRIEND'S DAY

1. Listen to her.
2. Ask her how you could help her.
3. Text her an encouraging Scripture verse.
4. Write her an uplifting note.
5. Leave a small "surprise" gift at her desk or locker.
6. Invite her over to spend the night.
7. Tell her something you like about her.
8. Smile really big when she walks in the door.
9. Sit beside her at lunch.
10. Include her in something you are doing with other friends.

A PROPER INVITATION

When we invite someone to something, we know there's always the risk of her saying no. Of course, nobody likes rejection; but on the other hand, who doesn't like to visit with her friend? So gather your courage, and try these simple suggestions:

- Explain what you have to offer first, then do the inviting.

  "My mom said I could invite a friend to go with us to the waterpark. Would you like to join us?"

- Be specific as to how she will get there and how she will get home. And, give her a specific time for arrival and departure.

  "My mom said she'd pick you up at nine in the morning and would bring you home about eight that night."

- Let her know any other important information, such as "be sure to bring a towel."

  "My mother said she'd buy your tickets, food, and all . . . but you might want to bring money if you want something from the gift shop."

- If she says yes, she'll probably need to ask her parents' permission and one of her parents might want to talk to one of your parents. So, give her some times when your parents might be available to answer questions.

- If she says no but doesn't give you a reason, do not ask why. Just say something such as, "I was hoping you could go. Maybe next time."

HOW TO DINE
WITH ROYAL SUCCESS

id you know that God wants His princesses to practice hospitality? One of the best ways we can host people in our homes and fellowship with our family is around the dinner table. Whether you are the host or guest, make sure you sharpen your royal table manners. You want everyone to come back for more—not head for the door!

So if you eat, or if you drink, or if you do anything,
do everything for the glory of God.

1 Corinthians 10:31

SIZZLING SERVICE

Think you're ready to call yourself a dining diva? Take this quiz to find out how hot your serving skills really are.

1. When the royal cook is preparing dinner, you . . .
   a. See what show you can watch on TV while ordering a pizza.
   b. Hang around the kitchen hoping to sample what she's making.
   c. Offer to help.

2. When asked to set the table, you . . .
   a. Pile flatware (forks, spoons, knives) and napkins in the middle of the table, then pray that someone else will arrange them properly.
   b. Put plates, forks, and napkins in their places on the table.
   c. Wipe the table clean. Then put plates, napkins, flatware, and glasses in their proper place on the table.

3. When arranging the table setting, you . . .
   a. Put the flatware on top of the plate.
   b. Put a fork and a spoon on the left, knife on the right.
   c. Put a fork on the left, then on the right put a knife next to the plate and a spoon next to the knife.

4. When everyone is called to dinner, you . . .
   a. Shout, "Hallelujah!" and start serving yourself.
   b. Wait until everyone is there and then start eating.
   c. Wait for everyone, and say a prayer of thanks to God. Then after everyone is served, you take your first bite.

5. When dinner is over, you . . .
   a. Jump out of your chair and run back to your TV show.
   b. Say "thank you" to whomever cooked the dinner and take your plate to the sink.
   c. Say "thank you" and then, when everyone is done, clear the table, and wash the dishes.

How's your dining etiquette?

Super-hot: If you answered **C** to most or all of the questions, you're really cookin' in the kitchen.

Simmering: If **b** seems more your style, you might want to step up your serving a notch.

Spoiled: If you chose **a** for most of the answers, turn up the heat by thinking of others more than yourself.

❓ WHAT'S WRONG WITH THIS PICTURE?

Her elbow is on the table.

PRINCESS MANNERS AT MEALTIME

As a child of God, you are His royal princess. But do you always act like one? Check out these princess pointers to polish your regal table manners.

Sitting pretty

Consider the chair your throne. You, as the princess, need to sit tall, one hand in your lap, and the other holding your fork or spoon. Your kingdom may crumble if you put your elbows on the table . . . well, perhaps not crumble, but shiver a little bit!

Table talk

Before you blurt out every detail of your day, slow down a bit so you can really talk—to God first and then to your family. Questions like, "What good thing happened to you today?" get lively conversations going. When others have finished talking, feel free to fill them in on your world.

Don't show and tell

Everyone wants to hear what you have to say, but not with food in your mouth! Wait until you swallow before gracing the world with your wisdom.

Pass perfection

When you need food that is out of reach, politely ask the person beside you to pass it. They'll gladly help, and you won't make a royal mess reaching over your plate!

Napkin no-nos

Suddenly, you realize more spaghetti sauce landed on your mouth than in it. What do you do? Not the tablecloth . . .

not the chair . . . not your arm . . . not your clothes or the curtain or a passing dog . . . But yes! Your napkin (which should be already neatly lying in your lap) is your best accessory for wiping your messy face.

Attitude of gratitude

Okay, not every meal will be your favorite. But a true princess is grateful for the food God provides and the cook who prepares it!

Helping hand

The meal is over, so now what? True leaders love to serve! Ask your hostess how you can help her clean the kitchen (and maybe she'll let you sneak a few scraps to the dog!).

> A princess takes a small, polite taste of food—
> unless she's allergic and would swell up like a puffer fish!

FIVE WAYS TO COMPLIMENT THE CHEF!

1. "This meal is awesome!"
2. "You're such a great chef!"
3. "Thank you so much for making this for us!"
4. "I've never had this before, but I'm sure it will be great because you made it."
5. "This is delicious!"

SETTING THE TABLE

There are all kinds of ways to set tables, from the casual everyday setting to an elegant royal event complete with fancy tablescapes—but there are certain rules everyone follows. First, before you set the table, clean it and remove any unappetizing items, such as your cat or pet turtle Walter. Add your tabletop decorations, which should be short enough that everyone can still see one another.

Informal
Set the table like this for every day. Did you notice a soup spoon, but the soup bowl is missing? It's because the soup will be served hot directly from the kitchen. If a soup bowl is present, most likely the soup will be served at the table.

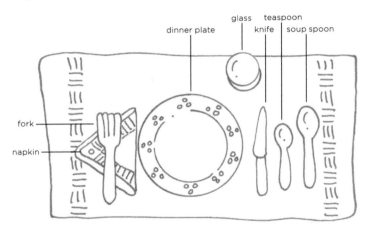

Formal
Going to a royal feast or a wedding, you might see lots of different flatware. Which do you use first? Usually, tables are set in the order you use the flatware, which means you should start with the flatware farthest from your plate. And as the meal progresses, more silverware and plates, bowls,

glasses, and cups might be brought to the table. Do not panic. Relax and follow the hostess's example to see how to use them. Above all, have fun!

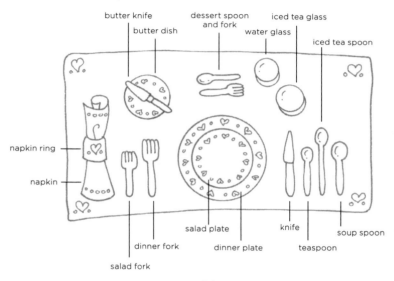

CUTTING UP

You're sitting still, tall, and quite regal. The food has been blessed and you're ready to begin. But before you can take a bite, you realize it's necessary that you cut the steak. To make matters worse, your bread needs buttering. And there's more than one knife and fork on the table. What's a princess to do?

Quick tips on proper cutting
- With the knife in your right hand and the fork in your left, run the blade just a little to the right of the fork. Carefully slice through the meat using as little of a sawing motion as possible. Cut only one small bite at a time.

- When you're ready to eat, put the knife down on the edge of the plate, keeping it off the table. Move the fork to your right hand and place your left hand back in your lap.

Bread basics
- When your server places a loaf of bread on the table, you may tear off a small portion and place it on your bread plate or on your dinner plate if a bread plate is not available.
- If there is a bread knife, you gently hold the sides of the loaf with your left hand. Then with the knife in your right hand, cut in a sawing motion letting the knife do the work. (Don't press down on the bread, or it will flatten and crumble.)
- Place your piece of bread on your plate, and pass the loaf or rolls to the left.

Butter, please
- Cut a slice of butter off using the butter knife. If there is no butter knife, cut it with an unused table knife. Place the pat of butter on your bread plate (if there is not a bread plate, use the edge of your dinner plate). Don't butter your bread using the butter knife! Pass the butter and butter knife to your left.
- To butter your bread, use your own knife and personal butter pat. Tear off a bite-sized piece of bread, butter it, and eat it. Repeat for each piece of bread.

A princess uses "May I have more, please?"
in her own or a friend's home,
but "I would like more, please." in a restaurant.

MAY I TAKE YOUR ORDER?

Take the challenge out of ordering food at a restaurant with these princess tips! (If you're a shy princess, practice ordering with your royal advisors before you go to the restaurant.)

- Before you select your food, make sure you brought enough money to cover the cost of the meal, plus the tip (unless it's a fast-food place). If you are with your royal advisors, be sure they approve of your choice.
- Take a few moments to read over the menu and make a selection. Save the chatting for after you've placed your order.
- When the server comes to your table, allow him or her to speak first. He may want to tell you about some specials of the day you'll want to consider, or he may want to take your drink order.
- When it's your turn to speak, look at your server and clearly tell him your order in a voice loud enough for him to hear, but quiet enough that everyone in the restaurant doesn't turn around and stare.
- Be sure to use "please" and "thank you." For example: "I would like some soda, please."
  "I would like the chicken linguini, please."
  "Would you suggest the super burrito or house nachos?"
- After you've ordered, smile, and say "thank you."
- Be patient. Remember that others are waiting to be served, as well.
- When the server returns with your food, keep your hands in your lap. Your server will place your plate in front of you.
- When you have been served, quietly say "thank you."
- Keep your glass away from the edge of the table.

SWEET OR SASSY

Pick your favorite foods from the lists below and find out how they reflect your personality!

1. Your favorite fruit is
   a. apples
   b. cantaloupe
   c. tangerines
   d. kiwifruit

2. If you had to order vegetables, you would choose
   a. broccoli
   b. mashed potatoes
   c. eggplant
   d. asparagus

3. Given a specific menu, you would want
   a. fish
   b. fried chicken
   c. spaghetti
   d. sushi

4. For dessert, you'd finish with
   a. a fruit cup
   b. banana pudding
   c. ginger snap cookies
   d. chocolate lava cake

5. If you had to choose a restaurant, it would serve
   a. healthy choices
   b. homestyle meals
   c. spicy foods
   d. the most unusual foods

If you picked mostly . . .

𝕒—You tend to be the quiet but determined type. You follow the rules and enjoy structure and lists. You wish you were more free-spirited like your friends, but teachers and parents appreciate your calm and collected presence in class and at home.

𝕓—You are a country girl at heart. Relaxed but hard-working, you find the fun side of life even in the middle of chores. You're dependable, though you will always choose being with friends over completing tasks.

𝕔—You love to be the life of the party. People rely on you to entertain and keep the conversation going. While everyone wants to be your friend, you still have a select group with whom you can truly relax. Your busy pace can wear people out, so be sure to stop every now and then to focus on what's most important in life.

𝕕—You have an eye for the unusual. Drawn to art, foods, and people who think out-of-the-box, you appreciate the creativity of God's creation. You can be moody and intense at times, but you think and feel deeply, which adds to your creativity. You like to spice life up with new adventures and experiences.

THE ETIQUETTE OF TEA

Tea time is an occasion to visit with friends. It can be a simple shared cup of tea with some snacks, a casual afternoon tea served in the living room with finger foods, or a fancy high tea served at a table with scrumptious courses of tiny sandwiches, sweets, and pastries. Princesses are most likely to serve or be served afternoon tea or high tea at a bridal shower or fund-raising event.

What a delicious way to practice your manners! Get with your royal advisors and invite some friends over. You may want to sample a few teas (hot and cold) and have some punch for the non-tea drinkers. For even more fun, think pink as your theme. To help get you started, try out these recipes.

Pink punch
Serves 5–6
½ gallon raspberry sherbet
1 liter bottle of a chilled lemon-lime-flavored,
    non-caffeinated soft drink
Optional: Fruit to add to cups

   Place sherbet in a punchbowl (or a large decorative bowl works too), pour the soft drink over it. Serve.

Berry delightful
Makes 4 half-cup servings
8 ounces of non-dairy frozen topping, thawed
1 small (serves 4) package of strawberry gelatin
Raspberries and/or strawberries, garnish

   Mix the non-dairy topping with dry granules of strawberry gelatin until well blended. Scoop spoonfuls of the strawberry mousse into clear dessert bowls or small glasses. Chill until set. Top with berries of your choice sliced or whole. Serve.

Pink cookies
Strawberry boxed cake mix (use dry)
½ cup butter or margarine, softened (not melted)
1 egg

   Put the dry cake mix in a large bowl. Add the butter and egg. Mix all with a mixer. Form into balls and place on cookie sheet. Bake at 375° for 8–10 minutes (depending on how soft or crispy you like them).

Now . . . put on your "pinking" caps and see what else you can dream up for your perfectly pink tea party!

A princess only chooses one item from each tray
at a tea. After everyone has been served,
she can choose one more item from each tray.

HOW TO POUR TEA

Pouring is done by the hostess, a close friend, or a royal advisor. And it's all about timing. With the tea cup to the side of the pot, carefully lift the pot with one hand while gently placing a finger or two on the lid of the pot to keep it in place. Place the pot's spout slightly above the cup. Tilt the pot so the tea pours. When the cup is a little less than three-fourths full, stop pouring. Put the pot down and pass the cup (and saucer if it has one) to the person who requested it.

HOW TO SPARKLE LIKE A PRINCESS

Being God's princess doesn't mean you have to be perfect. But there are some perfectly good pointers to help you act, look, and sound like a young lady whose presence and style leaves a sweet scent wherever she goes. When it's time for a polished appearance, try these trusted techniques. Your entire kingdom will thank you for it!

> *Our offering to God is this: We are the sweet smell*
> *of Christ among those who are being saved . . . .*
>
> 2 CORINTHIANS 2:15

FABULOUS TRESSES

Every princess wants to look and feel her best, and it starts with the simple ways we take care of ourselves. Turn these tips into habits, and you'll find the healthier, cleaner, and softer side of you.

Washing hair
- Make sure your hair is completely wet.
- Use about a quarter-sized amount of shampoo.
- Use your fingers to work the shampoo past the outside hair all the way to your scalp.
- Rinse with water until the slippery feeling is gone.

Adding some ease
Make your life—and brushing your lovely locks—easier by adding conditioner. Just follow the same steps for washing your hair. If your hair is really dry, start your bath or shower by washing and conditioning your hair. Leave the conditioner in for about three minutes or until just before you are ready to get out. Then rinse.

Taking the ouch out of tangles
- Hold your hair just above the tangle and gently comb the knot out, working from the bottom up.
- Gently separate the tangled hairs a few hairs at a time.

Drying dos and don'ts
- If you can, let your hair air-dry. It keeps your strands from splitting at the ends.
- If you need to blow-dry, start at the roots. Blow from back to front.
- Straighten or curl the outer layer of hair at the very ends.

Brushing hair

Unless your hair is braided or in a ponytail, comb or brush all your hair (including the back) several times. Once all the tangles are gone, style it with a part or add some fluff by brushing your hair back from your face.

BUBBLING WITH FUN

Have you ever experienced the luxury of a warm bubble bath . . . the kind with scented water, soothing sounds, and softening soap? If not, it's time to dip your toes into a new delight. (And if you want extra fun, re-create the experience for your mom or sister!)

✓ **What you'll need**
- [ ] bathrobe and slippers
- [ ] scented essential oil(s) or mint-scented shampoo
- [ ] music

1. Lay out your robe, slippers, and towel for when the bath is complete.
2. Fill the tub with almost hot water, adding scented shampoo or regular shampoo and scented oil as it fills.
3. Turn on a mix of soothing nature music, praise music, or nature sounds to play quietly in the background.
4. Dim the lights.
5. Then enjoy a quiet, peaceful soak in the tub. It's the perfect place to pray and relax.
6. When you're ready to get out, shower off all the bubbles.

Your towel, robe, and slippers are waiting!

PROTECT YOUR PRINCESS SMILE

Brushing is just the beginning. Be sure to clean the tops, bottoms, and sides of your teeth. Be sure to floss—while it may not be the highlight of your day, your teeth and gums will thank you for it. Finally, rinse well. And be sure to see a dentist for regular checkups to protect those pearly whites.

Love your lips
Don't neglect these little beauties. Put protective sunscreen on your face and lips before you leave for the day. At night, add a thin layer of petroleum jelly to your lips. By morning, your lips will be soft, smooth, and crack-free!

THE EDGE ON NAILS

Fingernails
You're too busy to bother with long, troublesome nails. Go with one of the two classic shapes—the squared or the rounded top—and keep your nails short.

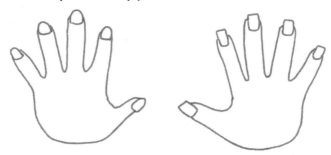

How to Be God's Little Princess

To get the squared-off look, file flat across the top of your nail. Angle the sides using the file, slightly rounding the edges.

For the rounded look, use a file beginning on one side. Use long strokes with the file, curving slightly in toward the center of the nail. Do the same on the other side. Finish by shaping the very top like an upside-down U.

Toenails

Do you have tough toenails? Find their softer side by soaking your feet in a warm saltwater solution. After about 5 minutes, remove one foot, dry it, and try clipping the edges first. Keep a file handy so you can smooth any edges, particularly around the sides where hangnails could occur. You'll have princess toes in no time.

DIVINE DESIGN

As a princess, you realize the importance of your fingernails and toenails looking nice all the time. And if you like to paint, they can become canvases for your creativity. Try out some of these nail painting techniques and tips, and you'll be ready to make ten (or twenty if you count toes) masterpieces!

✓ **What you'll need**
☐ fingernail polish remover (ask your royal advisor for help)
☐ cotton balls
☐ nail file
☐ nail brush
☐ fingernail paint, various colors (some nail art brands come with a super-tiny brush for detailed designs)
☐ bobby pin(s)

Prep the canvas

Remove any existing paint with a cotton ball and fingernail polish remover. Clean your nails by taking a bubble bath or soaking them in water and a little soap. Use a nail brush to get out that lovely gook that gets stuck under your fingernails (or toenails). Using the nail file, remove anything remaining under your nails.

Paint a basecoat

Use clear or any color you like. Let dry.

Creative touches

Polka dots. Dip the end of your bobby pin into a different colored paint. Carefully touch your nail with the painted bobby pin tip, then pull your hand straight up and off the nail. It should be a perfect dot! Continue painting as many dots of the same color as you want, or use more bobby pins with other colors to have a rainbow of fun.

Go for geometric designs. Using the paints with super-tiny brushes, try making zigzags down the center or side of your nail. Add just two or three simple dots with a bobby pin alongside the zigzag. Don't overdo it, or it will look too messy. Sharp and simple is the key.

Nail stickers. Dress up your nails fast with stickers featuring flowers, tiny gems, glitter, and other designs. For an artsy look, place the sticker off to one side. To keep stickers secure, paint a clear topcoat over the entire nail.

Break the Rules. Why limit yourself to just one color? Try a different shade on every nail surface. Or paint only half the nail one color, leaving the other half for something else. On game day, you can even paint them the colors of your favorite team!

FACE IT

Do you know how to wash your face? Is it with a washcloth, scrubbing hard? No! Be gentle with your complexion. Wash your face carefully, using only the tips of your fingers and a gentle soap recommended by your royal advisor. Rinse the soap off with lukewarm water, and pat dry with a soft towel.

A princess keeps her sunglasses
and eyeglasses sparkling clean.

SWEET SMELLS

Princesses do not sweat. Horses sweat, boys perspire, but girls—especially princesses—glow. The secret is to keep from glowing so much that all the flowers around you wilt from the smell.

But if you are starting to "glow" too much, don't despair. Girls' glistening is just God's creative way of cooling our bodies when we're overheated, and it also helps our bodies get rid of poisons that have built up in our blood.

Of course, just because it's functional doesn't make it something you want to show off. So how can we keep our fragrance fresh all day long? Try out these tips. They make good "scents."

- Bathe or shower frequently, being sure to rinse off all the soap.
- Dry off well. (If you don't need to dry off, pop back in the shower, and this time use water and soap.)
- Use a deodorant or antiperspirant.
- Drink a lot of water. The extra fluid helps your body stay cooler.

BEAUTY SLEEP

It may seem like an obstacle to fun, but sleep is really an important part of living well. Princesses know that sleeping helps keep their skin beautiful, gives their bodies time to refuel and rebuild muscle, helps their brains function better, triggers special growth hormones to help them be stronger and taller, and even helps them be in a better mood. That's why it's called *beauty sleep*. To get the most bang out of your zzz's, follow these steps to sounder sleep:

Create a good sleeping environment
Video games are fun, but they're not for bed. Keep your sleeping area cleared of anything that gets your brain excited instead of sleepy. Pick a pillow that's just right for you. If you must have noise, sound machines can create a white noise effect (like rain) that's perfect for tuning out other noises.

Make a relaxing bedtime routine
A routine tells your body it's bedtime. So find what works for you. It could be to wind down the day listening to soft music, reading your Bible or another book, or talking to God about your day.

Exercise early
If you wait too late to exercise, the adrenalin and other chemicals your body creates actually keep you from falling asleep.

Keep a healthy diet
Avoid sodas and other drinks with caffeine before bedtime. If you want a light bedtime snack, ask your royal advisors for suggestions.

Ways to fall asleep faster
- Actually get in bed.
- Listen to soft music.
- Read in bed.
- Think relaxing thoughts (picture the beach, the mountains, or your favorite relaxing spot).
- Turn on a fan or sound machine.
- Keep your room cool.

My royal notes:

_____

_____

_____

_____

_____

_____

HOW TO HAVE A ROCKIN' ROYAL PARTY

What's even better than being invited to the royal ball? Having one of your own, of course! It could be a slumber party, a swim party, a movie party, a costume party, or the all-time favorite a come-in-what-you-were-wearing-when-you-got-the-invitation party. Following are some good tips to help get you on your way to the gala of your dreams!

Always be happy.

1 Thessalonians 5:16

PLANNING THE PERFECT PARTY

Create an out-of-this world party your friends will remember by following these simple party planning must-dos.

Get organized
Grab a notebook, something to write with, and find a comfortable place to sit and think about your party.

Think theme
Dream about your perfect party. Whatever comes to mind, write it down. Ask your royal advisor to help. You two might even search online for party ideas. Write those ideas in your notebook too. Circle your top three ideas. With your royal advisor's advice, choose one idea.

Think budget and location
Yikes! Even royal ball's have budgets. But no matter how large or small the budget, great party planners think of creative ways to stretch it, such as making your own decorations or using a free location such as your home or a nearby park.

Think time, day, and dress
Will you have an after-school party or maybe something on a weekend afternoon or evening? How long will your party last? Will you have enough time to do everything you plan? What will you ask your guests to wear? Something formal, a swimsuit, pajamas?

Think details
- Whom will you invite?
- How will you transform the location into your dream theme?
- What type of food will you serve to match your theme?

- How many seats will you need? (Number invited + family + you = number of seats needed.)
- Which games will you play to start your guests talking and laughing?
- Will you be giving out store-bought or handmade party gifts, or have guests make a gift at the party?

INVITING INVITATIONS

It's fun to get an invitation! It's fun to send one too! You'll need to include the basics:

1. Type of party
2. Who is hosting
3. Where it will be
4. Time and date it will happen
5. Phone number to RSVP

(Want to really impress your friends? RSVP. stands for the French phrase *"répondez, s'il vous plaît,"* which means 'please reply' or 'respond, please'.)

Then start the party fun early by creating an invitation that is sure to get attention!

You can cut the invitations in the shape of your theme, go 3-D, or use simple objects to create an extra-special invitation. Just remember it needs to be slender enough to fit in an envelope, if you are mailing it. If you're handing out the invitation, have fun with the shape and style. Some ideas:

- A beach party's invitation could be shaped and colored like a beach ball—or written on a real beach ball.
- A slumber party's invitation could be in the shape of a star or crescent moon.
- Make a 3-D invitation by cutting a small square of double-sided foam tape to raise up whatever cut-out you want to stand up.
- Send your message in a bottle! Roll your invitation up like a scroll and place it in a small empty, clean, dry soda bottle. Add a little sand and either small shells or artificial flowers.
- Make a partially edible invitation. Bake miniature teacakes and wrap each individually in fabric or colored cellophane, tie with a ribbon, and attach your invitation.

MAKE IT AND TAKE IT

Have your guests create their own party favors. It's the perfect party project.

✓What you'll need
- ☐ a few potatoes
- ☐ 1 solid-colored T-shirt for each party guest
- ☐ fabric paints in various colors, including large and small tubes (for decorating details)
- ☐ fabric pens or Sharpie markers
- ☐ 1 square piece of cardboard as large as the T-shirt for each guest.
- ☐ a few sturdy plastic or foam plates
  Optional: fabric glitter and/or rhinestones, ribbon, fabric glue, glow-in-the-dark fabric paints, and glue-on items.

- Insert the cardboard inside the T-shirt.
- Cut the potatoes in half with a knife (might need Dad's help on that one).
- Squirt face-colored fabric paint onto the plates.
- Each guest (family members can do this too) dips the cut end of the potato into fabric paint and carefully makes one round paint print on her T-shirt.
- The girl then signs her name under the stamp print.
- When the paint and name are dry, each person decorates her own shirt.
- Once the paints and glue are dry, each girl passes her shirt around and each of the other girls autographs it.
- Each girl takes her shirt home as her party favor.

THE PATH TO PROPER INTRODUCTIONS

. . . But always try to do what is good
for each other and for all people.

1 THESSALONIANS 5:15

Not everyone at your party will know one another. Follow the flow chart to find the best way to introduce your friends.

- ↓ Your friends meet.
- ↓ You speak first.
- ↓ Talk directly to your friend: "Allison, I'd like you to meet Caitlyn."
- ↓ Look at your new friend. Call her by name: "Caitlyn, this is Allison."
- ↓ Tell your friend's story: "Caitlyn spent the week at summer camp with me. I asked her to hang out with us today."
- ↓ Introduce by name anyone else standing around.
- ↓ Think of a hobby or interest your new friend has in common with someone else in the group. Then start a conversation about it. Soon, your friend will feel comfortable enough to try new topics of her own.

A princess shows an interest in others.

CONVERSATION STARTERS

1. "Hi! My name is _____. What's your name?"
2. "Hey. How's it going?"
3. "What've you been up to lately?"
4. "Aren't you in my _____ class?"
5. "What did you do yesterday?"
6. "What are you doing during the holidays?"
7. "How did you like the movie _____?"
8. "Which computer game do you like best?"
9. "Where do you go to school?"
10. "You're new here. Where did you live before moving here?"

My royal notes:

_____

_____

_____

_____

_____

_____

_____

_____

_____

HOW TO BE MEDIA WISE

From texting to e-mails, computers and cell phones make communication easier than ever before. But watch out! Real dangers lurk in these kingdom parts. Sharpen your wits as you explore what technology has to offer.

Control yourselves and be careful! The devil is your enemy. And he goes around like a roaring lion looking for someone to eat.

1 Peter 5:8

PRINCESS PHONE MANNERS

When you talk, you should always be kind and wise. Then you will be able to answer everyone in the way you should.

COLOSSIANS 4:6

Are you the kind of princess who races to the phone, or would you rather just let it ring? If you tend toward the shy side, answering the phone might be a little intimidating, but it doesn't need to be. Just think for a moment, you get to play the part of both receptionist and ambassador by both fielding calls and delivering messages. All you need to remember are these helpful tips:

- If you have caller ID, remember that the machines don't know who is using the phone . . . they only recognize the phone number. Phones can be stolen. So be careful.
  - Only answer calls when you recognize the caller's number or name—and even then don't give your name out until you are sure it's the person you know who is calling.
  - If you don't recognize the caller's number or name, let the caller leave a message. If it's someone you know calling from a different phone, you can always pickup as they leave a message or return the call.

- Ask your parents what type of greeting they'd like you to use. Some families provide their last name, as in, "Hello, this is the _____ (say your last name) residence." Other families prefer to provide a name only if they know the person who is calling.
- If the person calling asks to speak to someone else, you could answer with any of the following:

- "Please wait just a moment and I'll find him/her." (If you recognize the caller.)
- "May I ask who's calling?" (If you don't recognize the caller.)
- "He/she cannot come to the phone right now. Would you like to leave a message?" Be sure to have a pen and paper ready so you can take down the caller's name, phone number, and a short message. Repeat the information to the caller. Follow-through by giving that person the message.

- If you are calling, always start by identifying yourself—even if you think the other person might recognize your voice.
  - "Hello, this is _____ (your name). Is _____ (your friend's name) able to talk right now? If the person answers yes, remember to say "thank you" as they go get the person you requested.
  - If the person you called isn't home, ask the person who answered, "May I leave a message, please?" If the person says yes, leave a message as described in the next section.

Leaving a message
Whether you get an answering machine, a message service, or a person is willing to take a message for you, you'll need to speak clearly and give the following information:

- ✓ your name,
- ✓ the name of the person you're trying to reach,
- ✓ a brief reason why you called, and
- ✓ a phone number where you can be reached.

Cell phone etiquette

Cell phones might seem cool, but being rude with them definitely isn't. A proper princess always remembers:

- to silence her phone whenever she's in church, class, a theater, or any other place where there is a need to keep quiet.
- to resist the urge to answer a call if she's already visiting with someone else. She knows she can call them back later.
- that time with friends and family is precious. She doesn't waste the moment by texting or playing games instead.

A princess gives her full attention to the people around her.

Wrong numbers and nosy callers

- Sometimes callers make mistakes and phone the wrong number. If that ever happens to you, simply say, "I'm sorry, but you have the wrong number," and hang up. If you're the caller who's made the mistake, tell them, "I called the wrong number. I'm so sorry to have bothered you."
- However, if a stranger calls and asks for your parents, never tell them if you are alone. Instead, say, "My parents are busy right now. May I take a message?"
- If a stranger calls, do not give out personal information, such as your name, address, family members' names, or if you are alone. Offer to take a message. If the person doesn't want to leave a message, hang up.

MAZE OF PHONE ANSWERS

Mark each quote below as true if it is an answer you should give; false if it is an answer you shouldn't give.

1. "What do you want?"
2. "Adams' residence."
3. "She's in the bathroom right now and it's not pretty."
4. "My parents aren't home right now."
5. "Yes, she's right here. Wait just a moment, please."
6. "I'm sorry, she can't come to the phone right now. Would you like to leave a message?"
7. "May I speak with Allison?"
8. "She's here somewhere. I'll yell for her."
9. "Would you take a message for me, please?"
10. "He's here, but he doesn't want to talk to you right now."
11. "I'm sorry, I called the wrong number."
12. "I'm too busy to go find her. Can you call back later?"
13. "HEY! I want to talk to Amy, NOW!"

Answers: 1-F, 2-T, 3-F, 4-F, 5-T, 6-T, 7-T, 8-F, 9-T, 10-F, 11-T, 12-F, 13-F

RU4 REAL?

Are you an Internet n00b? You know, someone who's new to the whole Internet and texting scene? If so, the following text talk notes might help.

tlk=talk
l8r=later
msg=message
lol=laugh out loud
jtlyk=just to let you know
fyi=for your information
ttyl=talk to you later
thx=thanks
np=no problem
bff=best friend forever
g2g=got to go
afk=away from keyboard
bbl=be back later
brb=be right back
rofl=roll on the floor laughing

Technology is opening new ways to communicate from across the sofa to around the world. Unfortunately, it's easy to start texting a phrase before knowing it means something bad, or to spend so much time chatting with cyber friends that the blessings of real-life relationships are missed.

As you enter this world of instant, anytime connection, keep these thoughts in mind:

- You represent Christ, no matter how you're doing the talking. Keep your talk God-honoring and pure.
- Work with your parents to set guidelines. How long should you spend on the Internet or phone? With whom are you allowed to speak? Which sites are okay to visit?
- It's easy to feel braver and surer of yourself when you don't have to look the person in the eye while you're speaking. In fact, you may be tempted to say a lot more than you ever would in person. Remember that the person on the other end is real and has real feelings, just like you.
- Electronics can seem intimidating. Ask for help.
- Remember that things from cell phones to the Internet open up new avenues for sharing the gospel right from your home!

INTERNET ARMOR

*. . . Wear God's armor so that you can
fight against the devil's evil tricks.*

EPHESIANS 6:11

The Internet can be used in many ways. International researchers can quickly share information, doctors can offer lifesaving treatments to people, missionaries can share God's Word, and friends can reconnect. That's all good, but the Internet is used in bad ways too. Some people scam kind-hearted people out of money, or pretend to be virtuous to trick you into telling where you live. So a wise princess needs to be on the lookout for danger. Use these tools to help protect yourself and your family:

Ask your parents to install Internet filters
Many different kinds are available for free, and others at a small yearly cost. It's worth every penny to prevent bad language or images from popping onto your screen, or from accidentally revealing where you live through hidden codes.

Start a secure blog or Web site with your parents' help
Keep safe by blogging only for friends and family, and by limiting access to your photos online.

Don't order anything online without your parents' help
Internet predators have very sneaky ways of getting your personal information, such as your phone number and street address. This also means they could steal your information or, worse, show up where you live.

Never give out your personal information
Ask your royal advisors to help you create a screen name—your own personal Internet nickname. And never tell people your full name, age, where you live, your phone number, your grade level, or the school or church you attend. Also, never tell them when your parents are gone, where you plan to go with friends, and never agree to meet them in person.

Don't believe everything you read
Just because you are an honest person doesn't mean that the stranger you're talking to online is. Stick to conversations with people you already know.

A princess doesn't post images of herself
in clothes she wouldn't wear in public.

INTERNET EXPERTISE

*Be wise in the way you act with people who are not
believers. Use your time in the best way you can.*

COLOSSIANS 4:5

Want to know how to be a real Internet pro? Learn these
dos and don'ts of online interactions.

Don't talk badly about other people (whether you know
them or not). In addition to it being just plain sinful, the
gossip will most likely get back to the other person.

Don't write messages when you're angry. You're much
more likely to say things you'll regret later when the
storm of emotions has passed.

Don't share your secrets on public forums like
Facebook and MySpace—or even in personal e-mails
to your friends.

Don't answer mysterious e-mails that pop up in your
inbox.

Don't click on any links in e-mails—even from people
you know. (Bad people called hackers can make phony
e-mails that look like they are from your friends.)

Don't look up a video on YouTube because your online
friend recommended it.

Don't argue or complain. Since the other person can't
read your facial expression or hear your tone, they
may totally misunderstand what you're trying to say.

Don't write or post anything or any picture you
wouldn't want the whole world—including Jesus—to
see. Because sooner or later, the whole world will see it.

Do use every opportunity you can to share your faith.

Do take a stand on issues that matter to God.

Do send encouraging e-mails to your friends.

Do post interesting facts.

Do connect with others in your class at school and church to deepen friendships.

Do use online connections to accomplish goals such as raising money for charities or finding sponsors for needy children, with help from your parents.

Do keep up with what's going on in the world. It's good to know where God is moving and which people and places need prayer at the moment.

REACHING OUT

Jesus said to the followers, "Go everywhere in the world. Tell the Good News to everyone."

MARK 16:15

The Internet makes it possible to reach the world right from your own home. So supporting God's missionaries is easier now than ever before. Following are just a few ways you can use the Internet's technology to share the good news of God's love with family and friends.

Keep in touch with missionaries

Lots of missionaries are getting in the technical groove and have begun posting e-newsletters to keep supporters informed. Ask your parents to help you decide on a missionary to support and make it part of your weekly or monthly routine to respond. Ask for prayer requests and tell them what God has been doing in your life. Your kindness will go a long way in encouraging them in their work.

Blog about your faith

If you like to write, consider blogging to be a blessing. Select meaningful Bible verses and post them on your secure site. Record how you see God's hand at work in your life. Invite your family and friends to read your site.

Share God's love through poems and music

Are you a poet or songwriter? The Internet makes it easy to post your compositions for family and friends. Just think, you could lead people to Christ.

Encourage your friends

The Bible says that we need to stay close to other believers and encourage them every day until Christ comes back. It only takes a minute to shoot an encouraging e-mail out to your friends. Sites such as www.biblegateway.com have a Bible verse of the day. You could use it as the inspiration for an encouraging e-mail. Following are some phrases to consider:

- "I was thinking about you today."
- "I'm praying for you too."
- "I'm thanking God for you today"
- "You are such a blessing to me. Thanks for your friendship."
- "Isn't God great?! I'm so glad He had me meet you."
- "I can't wait to see what great things God has planned for you today."

PRINCESS WORD SEARCH

Find the words below in the puzzle and circle them. One is done for you.

```
W   W   O   H   P   Q   E   L   H   P  (E   L   I   M   S)
C   H   P   U   T   R   B   F   R   I   D   N   L   F   Y
V   O   C   I   U   B   L   I   Y   F   B   T   M   R   W
Z   B   A   T   F   Q   N   I   T   U   C   X   M   G   H
A   R   S   G   V   C   A   E   G   R   Z   S   J   Y   R
A   O   T   H   E   F   X   T   V   I   U   W   X   H   J
P   Q   K   S   S   R   I   Z   A   G   U   Q   U   R
V   B   S   I   C   W   A   Q   I   P   R   Y   O   A   K
S   N   R   E   T   H   G   U   A   D   O   T   Z   C   K
Y   R   W   J   H   G   U   E   C   J   F   L   J   M   G
X   J   E   L   R   U   F   T   C   O   S   A   I   W   D
U   L   Q   N   O   X   F   T   A   R   X   Y   B   T   B
A   V   W   U   N   L   B   E   W   I   P   O   O   W   E
C   F   V   Y   E   A   O   W   B   Y   R   R   P   X   Q
G   D   Y   S   R   E   M   B   E   A   U   T   Y   Y   M
```

BEAUTY	DAUGHTER	ETIQUETTE
GIGI	MANNERS	POLITE
POSTURE	PRINCESS	ROYALTY
✓ SMILE	THRONE	TIARA

See answer page 94.

INTERNET RESOURCES

Games

http://www.TommyNelson.com/free-goodies
http://Christiankidstop100.com

Information and links to literally 100 different Christian sites packed with fun games, devotionals, and tools for learning.

Bible study resources

Each of these sites helps you search the Scriptures in a wide variety of translations. They can also point you to other sources for deeper Bible understanding.

http://Kidsbible.com
http://Biblestudytools.com
http://Bible.com
http://Biblegateway.com

My royal notes:

_____

_____

_____

_____

_____

_____

_____

Princess Word Search Answer

```
W  W  O  H  P  Q  E  L  H  P  E  L  I  M  S
C  H  P  U  T  R  B  F  R  I  D  N  L  F  Y
V  O  C  I  U  B  L  I  Y  F  B  T  M  R  W
Z  B  A  T  F  Q  N  I  T  U  C  X  M  G  H
A  R  S  G  V  C  A  E  G  R  Z  S  J  Y  R
A  O  T  H  E  F  X  T  V  I  U  W  X  H  J
P  Q  K  S  S  S  R  I  Z  A  G  U  Q  U  R
V  B  S  I  C  W  A  Q  I  P  R  Y  O  A  K
S  N  R  E  T  H  G  U  A  D  O  T  Z  C  K
Y  R  W  J  H  G  U  E  C  J  F  L  J  M  G
X  J  E  L  R  U  F  T  C  O  S  A  I  W  D
U  L  Q  N  O  X  F  T  A  R  X  Y  B  T  B
A  V  W  U  N  L  B  E  W  I  P  O  O  W  E
C  F  V  Y  E  A  O  W  B  Y  R  R  P  X  Q
G  D  Y  S  R  E  M  B  E  A  U  T  Y  Y  M
```

HOW TO BE A PERFECTLY POLITE PRINCESS

What's the point in being polite? you may secretly wonder to yourself. Well, manners and etiquette are guidelines that help you to make good decisions in all types of situations. And, by using them, you can show the love of Christ in every aspect of your life.

> *Remind the believers to do these things: to be . . . ready*
> *to do good, to speak no evil about anyone, to live in*
> *peace with all, to be gentle and polite to all people.*
>
> Titus 3:1–2

A PRINCESS SHOWS RESPECT

A princess is respectful—even when she doesn't want to be.

A princess knows the importance of honoring others by showing respect to those around her—including her parents and other family members—even when she might be angry with them. You can show honor to the people around you by following these dos and don'ts.

Do address adults with respect. (Don't call them by their first name unless they've asked you to do so; instead, use a title in front of their last name: Mr. Harris, Miss Holt, Mrs. Morgan.)

Do make your answers yes or no, not yeah.

Do ask others politely for help, but don't demand help.

Do offer adults your chair when there's nowhere for them to sit.

Do ask for permission.

Do obey those in charge.

Do look for ways to be helpful with carrying packages, groceries, suitcases, and so forth.

Do always say thank you for gifts—even if it is something you don't like.

Don't be sarcastic or disrespectful when talking.

Don't sigh or moan when asked to do something.

Don't interrupt when someone else is talking.

Don't demand your own way.

Don't roll your eyes.

THE ART OF ASKING PERMISSION

*Children, obey your parents the way the Lord
wants. This is the right thing to do.*

EPHESIANS 6:1

You want your friend to come over to work on a school project; however, you know your parents prefer to keep things quiet during the school week. What's the best way for a poised princess to respectfully put forth her royal request? Follow these dos and dont's, and your request might be granted.

Don't ask while your parent is on the phone.
Don't ask them while your friend is standing right there.
Don't tell them what you're going to do without asking at all.
Don't tell them that everybody else's parents let them.
Don't throw yourself on the floor and have a temper tantrum.
Don't be disrespectful.
Don't ask your other parent when the first one says no.

Do approach them with respect.
Do ask them when it is quiet and others aren't around.
Do start your question, "Would it be okay if . . . ?"
Do include in your question any information they might need to know. "Samantha and I are working on a school project together. Would it be okay if . . . ?"

A princess doesn't slam doors.

The real delight comes from your attitude in the asking. If you trust your parents and respect their authority—even if their decision goes against your wishes—you will gain their respect and trust. If you argue and complain, they will be even less likely to listen—and it will hurt your relationship with them.

PRINCESS BLUNDER BAND-AIDS (RIGHTING WRONGS)

But if we confess our sins, he will forgive our sins. We can trust God. He does what is right. He will make us clean from all the wrongs we have done.

1 JOHN 1:9

Did you just blow it? A heartfelt apology can go a long way toward mending a friendship. And many times your friend will want to forgive you. She might even feel partially responsible and ask for your forgiveness too. Following are some ways you might start your apology:

- "Wow! I can't believe I just did that. Will you forgive me?"
- "You're right. I'm wrong. Will you forgive me?"
- "I had no idea I hurt you! Will you forgive me?"
- "Sometimes I can be so self-centered. Will you forgive me?"
- "I don't know what comes over me sometimes. Will you forgive me?"

> A princess understands that God knows when an apology is heartfelt.

No matter what you choose to say, *how* you say it is the key. Be sincere in your apology. Show you mean it by asking her to forgive you and then try not to do again what upset your friend. In your humble response, she'll see the love of Christ.

WHAT'S WRONG WITH THIS PICTURE?

"What happened?"

"Well, sorry! You care too much about clothes!

It is not a heartfelt apology.

We serve a great God who is full of love, compassion, and forgiveness. Next time you make a mistake, turn to your heavenly Father for help and forgiveness. He gives it freely and full of His love!

SO SORRY!

Have you ever been in a fight with anyone? How did it end? Maybe someone came in and made you say "I'm sorry" to the other person, or made her say she was sorry to you. Or maybe both of you had to apologize. Did you know that God tells His people to say "I'm sorry" too? He isn't interested in your doing it because you're in trouble, though. God wants us to repent from our hearts so we can stay close to Him.

So what is *repentance*? Sometimes it helps to see what it isn't so you can know what it is. Can you tell which is true repentance and which is fake repentance?

1. Saying you're sorry, but continuing to do the wrong thing.
2. Admitting that what you did was wrong.
3. Feeling sorry for what you did.
4. Shifting the blame to another person.
5. Praying for strength not to do it again.
6. Pretending like you never did anything wrong.
7. Accepting the blame without pointing to someone else.
8. Pretending it was just a joke gone wrong.
9. Turning from that sin and turning to God.
10. Asking God for forgiveness.

Answers: 1-F, 2-T, 3-T, 4-F, 5-T, 6-F, 7-T, 8-F, 9-T, 10-T.

How to Be God's Little Princess

Real repentance is a gift from God. It's a change of heart that only comes when we ask Him for it. So if you don't feel sorry, pray for help! God promises to forgive us instantly when we confess our sins to Him. He will never hold it against us!

SINCERELY YOURS

I am Paul, and I end this letter now in my own handwriting.
All my letters have this to show they are from me. . . .

2 THESSALONIANS 3:17

You can e-mail or even text a note in seconds, but there is something personal about a handwritten letter that can't be captured by a computer. When you take the time to handwrite a note of encouragement or thanks, the recipient knows you spent something more valuable than money on them. You took time to share your heart with them, and they'll treasure your kindness.

Create extra flair while sending thoughts of love by making your own stationery. Check out the Internet for ideas.

THE "WRITE" WAY

Every gift we receive comes from God. It's just that He often uses other people to carry His blessings to us.

Learning how to say thanks to God is really important! One of the ways we can start to grow a thankful heart is by noticing all the kind things people do for us and thank them. Of course, you should always say thank you to them right away, but when you follow it with a well-written, thank you note, it strengthens your gratitude and will be a blessing to them, as well.

To write a well-rounded, thank you letter include:

1. Date
2. Person you are thanking.
3. What you are thankful for
4. Why you are thankful
5. Thank them again for the gift
6. Choose a closing phrase
7. Sign it by hand

August 11, 2011 ——— 1
Dear Mrs. Foster, ——— 2

3 ——— Thank you so much for remembering my birthday. The necklace you gave me is beautiful! I love to wear it with my dresses. You are always so thoughtful. I also love the way ——— 4 you make me laugh when we come to visit you. Thanks for being a good friend to my family and me. And thanks again for the necklace!

5

Love, ——— 6
Samantha ——— 7

For a younger friend, you might write:

August 11, 2011 ——— 1
Hi Maddie! ——— 2   3

Thank you for inviting me to your home this weekend and taking me to the state fair. I always have so much ——— 4 fun with you! The candied apples were pretty awesome too. You're such a great friend. I'm so thankful that God brought us together. Thanks again for the great weekend. Have a wonderful day!

5

Blessings, ——— 6
Samantha ——— 7

How to Be God's Little Princess

HOW TO BE
A PRINCESS AT HOME

Princesses are recognizable without a tiara by the way they show kindness to others—and that includes their family members. In this section, you'll find simple steps to help you plan your day, get along with others in your family, and care for your pets.

Do what is right to other people. Love being kind to others. And live humbly, trusting your God.

MICAH 6:8

WHERE'D THE TIME GO?

There is a right time for everything.
Everything on earth has its special season.

ECCLESIASTES 3:1

A princess uses her time wisely.

However you slice it, God says we need to spend our time wisely. He even tells us that the more time we spend with Him, the more beautiful our hearts become. But sometimes we don't even know where the time goes! Look at where you spend most of your time. Record how many hours you spend on each activity. Then create your own pie chart like the one on this page (it can be larger or smaller than this one). Color in the pie chart using colored pencils or pens. Use a different color for each activity. For example, if you spend an hour and a half on homework, color in one-and-a-half slices in yellow on the pie chart.

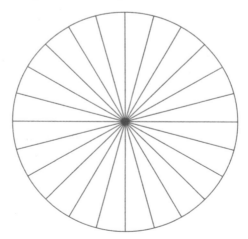

Sleeping (red):___
Eating (green):___
Time with God (blue):___
Schoolwork (yellow): ___
Watching TV (purple): ___
Standing on your head (aqua):___
Computer/video games (black): ___
Phone (brown):___
Outdoor activities (orange): ___
Serving others (pink): ___
Chores (lime):___

Look at your pie chart. How much is blue compared to the rest? How much pink? Do you need to make any changes to the way you spend your day?

CATCHING TIME

Do not worry about anything. But pray and ask
God for everything you need. And when you pray,
always give thanks. And God's peace will keep
your hearts and minds in Christ Jesus. . . .

PHILIPPIANS 4:6–7

You'll have more time for fun, if you work with your royal advisors to develop a schedule and checklist. Use a calendar or day planner (create your own by decorating a notebook), and write in it everything you need or want to do. Allow time for your chores, but time to play too. Remember to allow travel time. If you leave your youth group at 3:00, you probably won't be home for piano practice at 3:01. Try these simple princess techniques to help your day go smoothly.

Plan ahead

Don't wait until the alarm goes off or the doorbell rings. Plan what you want to wear and lay it out neatly near your bed or in your closet. Make sure you have your jewelry, shoes, purse, and book bag ready too!

Write your routine

Make a checklist of your routine, tape it to the mirror or door, and follow it. (Be sure to include anything you might need that day.) Your early morning, school day checklist might look something like this:

- ☐ Time with God
- ☐ Shower
- ☐ Put on deodorant
- ☐ Fix hair
- ☐ Get dressed
- ☐ Eat breakfast
- ☐ Brush teeth and hair
- ☐ Get book bag
- ☐ Remember lunch or lunch card or money
- ☐ Hug Mom and Dad
- ☐ Go!

Congratulations! You've made it to school (or wherever you were headed) on time, dressed, with good breath, and smelling sweet. Now smile, you're ready for anything!

Where'd the time go?

After you've created and worked with your schedule a few weeks, go back and fill out the pie chart again under "Where'd the Time Go?" on page 104. Is it different this time? How did it change?

THE SECRET TO LOVING SISTERS AND BROTHERS

Do everything without complaining or arguing.

PHILIPPIANS 2:14

God has called each one of us to be peacemakers, and He wants our families to be full of His love. Yet Christians everywhere struggle to live peacefully with their family members—especially when it's a brother or sister. So what's a princess to do?

God is in control
God hand-picked your family for you—and yes, that includes your brother(s) and/or sister(s). Remember, when you choose to treat them well, you are honoring God.

Love one another
When Jesus said to love every person on earth, He meant your family members too. No matter what annoying thing they do, Jesus says to pray for them and love them in return.

It's all in the family
Your brothers and sisters are also your brothers and sisters in Christ. God has plans for them, just as He has for you. So you need to show them the kind of respect you'd expect to find in a royal family.

Remember your own faults
No one is perfect, not even you. But remember that your family loves you anyway. Try to use your best manners all the time. Say thank you and please, and ask before you borrow anything.

Show Kindness

When your brother or sister is getting on your last nerve, take a deep breath and slowly let it out as you try to find a way to be the peacekeeper and avoid a fight. Remember, Jesus said that however we treat the people here on earth is how we treat Him. Let's love Jesus well by loving our family well.

FAMILY OUTINGS

Check off your favorites. Then get with your royal advisors and plan some fun outings with your family.

- ☐ Bike riding
- ☐ Bowling
- ☐ Camping
- ☐ Canoeing
- ☐ Church activity
- ☐ Fishing
- ☐ Garage sales
- ☐ Going out for ice cream
- ☐ Hiking
- ☐ Ice or roller skating
- ☐ Visits to the library
- ☐ Miniature golf
- ☐ Going to a movie
- ☐ Nature walks / Park trips
- ☐ School football game
- ☐ Star gazing
- ☐ State fair
- ☐ Volunteering
- ☐ Walk around the neighborhood

PET PROJECT

Do you have any pets at home? If so, you have a chance to practice true princess care for some subjects who can't serve themselves. Think about it. Your pets look to you like any loyal peasant would. It's up to you to love them, feed and water them, and create a place where they love to play. Following are some fun ways to give your pets the attention they need.

Make a pet center
Clear out some space in your laundry room, garage, or wherever your royal advisors direct. Keep all your pet care products neatly organized on a shelf or in a bucket. You can even use labels so everyone knows where to put the leashes, litter, food, treats, shampoo, brushes, toys, and other pet items.

Make a pet plan
Map out your week. Which day should you clean the fish tank? Walk the dog? Change out the cat litter box? Spread out the big chores throughout the week, but put daily reminders on the chart to fill the food and water bowl.

Use pet etiquette

Yes, there is etiquette for pets. But a princess knows she's in charge of her pets. So when friends come over: Introduce your pet (but if guests don't want to pet your alligator, don't make them); keep pets from jumping or tripping anyone; keep pets safe and away from things like flying baseball bats; show kindness when the pet wants to play too.

Have fun with your pets

Pets are fun. And your pets will adore you if you take time to play with them. And guess what—you can teach them some manners (as well as really cool tricks) while you are playing with them. So, put aside the computer and phone and have fun with your loyal subjects!

HOW A PRINCESS SPORTS A GOOD ATTITUDE

Every princess needs to leave the palace luxury long enough to get her heart pumping, blood flowing, and body working. Exercise also brings an opportunity for grace—the kind of attitude that celebrates the sport and all those who play it.

All those who compete in the games use strict training. They do this so that they can win a crown. That crown is an earthly thing that lasts only a short time. But our crown will continue forever.

1 CORINTHIANS 9:25

RANK YOUR HEALTH

What's your health rating? Do you treat your body like a temple or like a junkyard? Take this quiz to find out.

1. You're tired. You come home and immediately grab a snack before you collapse in front of the TV. You choose . . .
   a. an apple
   b. chips
   c. peanuts
   d. candy

2. You've just woken up and you're starving. You head for the fridge to find some breakfast. You choose . . .
   a. yogurt
   b. leftover pizza
   c. eggs
   d. donuts

3. You suddenly feel very thirsty and realize you haven't had a drink all day. You decide to drink . . .
   a. milk
   b. soda
   c. water
   d. lemonade

4. You're at a buffet-style restaurant and your royal advisor requests you choose healthy foods. You pile your plate with . . .
   a. baked fish, green beans, and apples
   b. macaroni and cheese, mashed potatoes, and onion rings
   c. grilled chicken kabobs, whole-grain rice, tomato slices
   d. ribs, baked beans, and french fries

PRETTY TOUGH

You're torn. You like to dress up, look pretty, and do the girl thing—but your tomboy side loves to discover insects, catch minnows, and explore all of God's creation. To top it off, you can play sports with the boys and win. And so you wonder, *Is that okay?*

Yes! God created His girls to be as well-rounded as they can be. He loves it when we love the life He's given us. The key is keeping a proper balance. Remember:

- Girls and boys ARE different. Boys think and act differently from girls—even tomboyish girls.
- Don't give up being girly just to be with the boys. You can enjoy sports or other interests without losing your girly side. For example, you can still wear earrings and your hair in an updo while you go fishing with your dad and brothers.
- God made both boys and girls with His glory and purpose in mind—and both boys and girls are greater because of it.

A princess knows that if she's honoring God
and her parents, then she's free to
express herself the way God made her to be.

SWIMMING ETIQUETTE

A princess doesn't swim alone.

Poolside manners

Different pools have different rules. You'd be wise to read them or ask the owner before you take that first dive. But no matter where you stop to soak your toes, keep a close watch on these pool dos and don'ts:

Do pull back long hair in a ponytail or braid(s).

Do use your own towel, not the one closest to you.

Do always have an adult with you before entering the pool.

Do rinse off before you enter the pool.

Do avoid jumping on or near people when you make your grand entrance.

Do know how deep the water is before you jump or dive in.

Do put any equipment or toys that you borrowed back where they belong.

Do dry off before entering a car, building, or home.

Do put a dry towel on the car seat before sitting down.

Do drink plenty of water.

Do wear sunscreen for outside activities.

Don't whack other swimmers with toys or flotation devices.

Don't run on the pavement. It's swimming, not racing, after all—and pavement is slippery when wet, making it easy to fall.

Don't dive into shallow water. Too many people who ignore this rule end up seriously injured.

How to Be God's Little Princess

Don't play in areas where people are diving or sliding into the water.

Don't sit on inside furniture in a wet swimsuit.

Don't bring breakable dishes or glass to the pool area. (Choose plastic cups and plates, instead.)

WHAT'S WRONG WITH THIS PICTURE?

By yelling, she is not following proper game etiquette.

GAME ETIQUETTE

God says that whatever we do, we do it for His glory. But when it comes to sports, our trying to win can get in the way. It's easy to want to win so much, we throw our royal manners out the window. Don't lose your royal head. Remember these little rules for playing well, and you'll win a good reputation no matter how the game turns out.

A princess treats others as she would like to be treated!

Do use deodorant or antiperspirant before you work out.

Do listen to your coach's or teacher's instructions.

Do offer to help others learn the game.

Do ask before you join a game. (If someone asks to join your game, let them.)

Do participate in the team by doing your best—even if it's not what you do best.

Do be kind to those who aren't as skilled as you are.

Do be nice whether you win or lose.

Do take turns.

Don't make loud grunts—even if you are working hard.

Don't walk in front of mirrors and block someone who is correcting her position.

Don't use equipment you are not trained to use.

Don't talk about how great you are or how much better you are than your opponent.

Don't use heavy equipment without an adult present.

Don't break the rules of the game.

Don't yell at someone for making a bad play.

Don't call someone a cheater.

CHAMPION ATTITUDE

Pride leads only to shame. It is wise not to be proud.

PROVERBS 11:2

When you win, do you like to show off like some star athletes, or do you prefer quiet applause? Even more important is your attitude when you lose. To keep your royal sweetness, whether you win or lose, keep these tips in mind:

Winning is more fun than losing
A lot of times you just feel better about yourself if you win. But it's God who makes us great, not our gifts or talents.

Go for the glory
God's glory, that is. Keep reminding yourself that the real prize comes when you honor God—win or lose.

Competing thoughts
In order to win, you have to think of ways to beat the competition. You plan, prepare, and pile on your best efforts. When the game or competition is over: **Keep calm. Keep it nice. Keep it real**. And remember, whether you are good at sports or your talent is in something else—such as music, math, writing, or photography—be kind because God has given everyone a different gift.

Things to say—win or lose
At a loss of words after the final score? Practice with your royal advisors what to say and do, whether you win or lose.

When you win, you might say:

- "That was a good game."
- "You would make a good cheerleader too."

When you lose—even though you might be sad—you could say:

- "You did a great job!"
- "Congratulations, your routine was really good."

Winning isn't everything

We learn from both our mistakes and our victories. So next time you flub, don't get flustered. Remember that God will use it to make you even stronger and wiser next time!

HOW A PRINCESS KNOWS SHE NEEDS AN INNER BEAUTY MAKEOVER

What does God see when He sees your heart? Are you kind and thoughtful or mean and selfish? God designed our hearts to be beautiful. He wants our inner qualities—such as gentleness, self-control, kindness, and patience—to reflect His love to all those around us.

It is not fancy hair, gold jewelry, or fine clothes that should make you beautiful. No, your beauty should come from within you—the beauty of a gentle and quiet spirit. This beauty will never disappear, and it is worth very much to God.

1 PETER 3:3–4

INNER BEAUTY

The Spirit gives love, joy, peace, patience, kindness,
goodness, faithfulness, gentleness, self control. . . .

GALATIANS 5:22–23

You probably know more about inner beauty than you think. Try the matching quiz below to see how well you do. Match the words in the first list with the qualities the princess is showing in the second list.

- Love
- Joy
- Peace
- Patience
- Kindness

- Goodness
- Faithfulness
- Gentleness
- Self-control

A princess . . .

a. Laughs with happiness as she and a friend take turns flying a kite.
b. Is splashed with mud, but does not get angry.
c. Does not cheat on her schoolwork.
d. Hugs her mother.
e. Invites a new student to join her for lunch.
f. Waits her turn in a long line, without complaining.
g. Doesn't worry when unexpected things happen.
h. Chooses to go to worship service instead of going shopping at the mall.
i. Tenderly cleans her little brother's scraped knee.

Answers: A-joy, B-self-control, C-goodness, D-love, E-kindness, F-patience, G-peace, H-faithfulness, I-gentleness

BEAUTY AID

Charm can fool you, and beauty can trick you. But a woman who respects the Lord should be praised.

Have you noticed how people can change before your eyes by the way they act? Maybe you thought someone was beautiful, and then you saw her bully someone. Suddenly, she's not so pretty anymore? Or maybe someone you've never considered beautiful does something kind to help another person. Which of the two girls has true beauty?

How beautiful is *your* heart? Do you frown a lot? Do you feel grumpy? Do you do unkind things? Do you need a heart makeover? God is the only beauty specialist you'll need, because beauty comes from the inside out. Start your heart makeover by living every day in a way that reflects God's love for you. Before long, those around you will begin to see a change in your outer appearance. That old grumpy you will begin to change into a new, joyful, glowing, and beautiful you. Just remember a beautiful heart . . .

- Treats others the way you want them to treat you.
- Honors and respects God, parents, others, and yourself.
- Wants to dress modestly.
- Is honest and trustworthy.
- Looks for ways to help those in need.
- Wants to make a difference.
- Offers comfort when unfortunate things happen.
- Loves God with all her might.
- Wants to learn more about God's ways.
- Communicates with God in prayer.
- Trusts God when things go wrong.

A GIFT FROM GOD

For God loved the world so much that he gave his only Son. God gave his Son so that whoever believes in him may not be lost, but have eternal life.—John 3:16

WHAT'S WRONG WITH THIS PICTURE?

The girls are not being respectful to those around them.

BEAUTY ESSENTIALS

*I have taken your words to heart so I
would not sin against you.*

PSALM 119:11

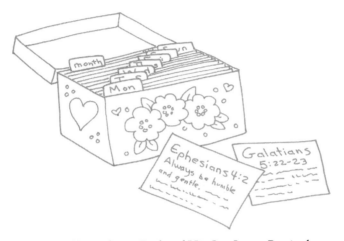

The Bible tells us about God and His Son Jesus. But it also provides wisdom and comfort. A princess memorizes Scripture to carry God's Word in her heart at all times. To help you memorize Scripture, you can create your own Beauty Box that's packed with God's powerful promises and guidelines. Just follow these easy steps to hiding God's Word in your heart.

✓ **What you'll need**
- [ ] recipe box
- [ ] 3x5 lined note cards, any color
- [ ] 9 blank divider tabs
- [ ] colored markers
- [ ] stickers
- [ ] pencil or pen

Decorate your recipe box. Be sure to put your name on it. Include your favorite verse or its reference. Use stickers or colorful tape or whatever you want to make it yours.

1. Label your tabs.
   - Label the first 7 tabs Monday, Tuesday, Wednesday, Thursday, Friday, Saturday, and Sunday.
   - Label tab 8: Monthly review.
2. Place extra blank cards in the back of your box so that you can make more verse cards when you're ready.
3. Copy one Bible verse on a blank card. Place it behind Monday.
4. On Monday, take out the Bible verse, read it and repeat it to yourself. Close your eyes and try to say it again. You may want to try writing it out without looking. When you are through, place it behind Tuesday.
5. On Tuesday, try to say the verse without looking at it. Then take it out, read it, and see how much you remembered. Close your eyes and try to say it again from memory. When you are through, put it in the box behind the label Wednesday. Repeat this each day through Friday, always putting the card behind the next day when you are through.
6. Save Saturday and Sunday for review. If you remember the verse, put the card behind the label for the monthly review.
7. On Monday, if your memory is a little shaky, spend more time on the verse from the previous week. If you have it memorized, start with a new verse.
8. At the end of the month, review all four of your verses and see how many you can say from memory.
9. The next month, repeat from number three to number eight of this list. By the end of the year, you will have learned 52 verses. That's really great!

Some verses you might like to include: John 3:16; Mark 16:15; Proverbs 3:4, John 1:1; Revelation 3:20; Psalm 139:1; Psalm 139:2; Psalm 139:3; Psalm 139:4; Psalm 139:5.

LIVING THE PRINCESS LIFE

Now that you know the secrets to being a perfectly polite princess—use them to allow God's glory to shine through you. Go forth with confidence that you know how to . . .

☐ live like the daughter of the King of kings.
☐ let your actions show your true beauty.
☐ dress like a princess.
☐ improve your poise.
☐ be friends princess style.
☐ make a heartfelt apology.
☐ dine with royal success.
☐ sparkle like a princess.
☐ host a party.
☐ be media wise.
☐ be perfectly polite.
☐ act like a princess everywhere— even at home.
☐ sport a good attitude.

ALWAYS A PRINCESS

You started this book by looking in a mirror to find a princess—and it was you! Now look again: there sits a wiser princess before you now—and it is you! And as gorgeous as you are now, your beauty does not even compare with the beauty you'll see when God is finished fashioning your heart.

That's right: God is working in your life right now—even as you read this—to make you into the most beautiful princess imaginable. No matter where you live, or what your age, or what is happening in your life—God will always be there for you, and He will always love you. There will be moments when you feel alone or misunderstood, you will have good days and bad days. But no matter what is going on your heavenly Father delights in you. My prayer is that you will celebrate the girl you see in that mirror. You are God's beautiful, incredible princess—a crowning jewel in His kingdom.

Sheila Walsh

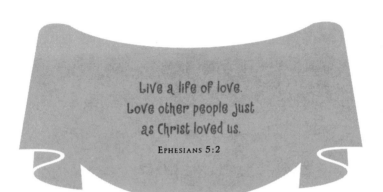

Live a life of love.
Love other people just
as Christ loved us.

EPHESIANS 5:2